I0823055

C P

# Wall Flowers

## A LOVE LETTER TO WALLPAPER

**ELIZABETH REES**
*founder of* CHASING PAPER

with Stephanie Sisco ⁜ Photography by Anna Spaller

Gibbs Smith

PHOTOGRAPHY CREDITS

Carmel Brantley: 154
Donna Dotan/Trunk Archive: 164–67, 173
Kerry Kirk Photography: 212, 218–22
Mayo Studios: 136–45, 151
Finn McClendon: 146
Read McKendree/JBSA: 158–59, 169
Elizabeth Rees: 24, 28, 29, 31
Anna Spaller: 8, 11, 12, 25, 27, 28, 30, 32–43, 45–71, 76–91, 94, 99, 102–9, 112, 120, 125–29, 160–63, 170–71, 176–91, 194–209, 216, 225–26
Stefano Ukmar: 134
Sarah Voigt Photography: 116–19, 130–31
Phil Walters: 31
Jenni Yolo: 96–97, 100

First Edition
30 29 28 27 26     5 4 3 2 1



Published by
Gibbs Smith
570 N. Sportsplex Dr.
Kaysville, Utah 84037
www.gibbs-smith.com

The authorized representative in the EEA is Simon and Schuster Netherlands BV, Herculesplein 96 3584 AA Utrecht, Netherlands, info@simonandschuster.nl

Designed by Sheryl Dickert
Printed and bound in China

Library of Congress Control Number: 2025938805

ISBN: 978-1-4236-6791-9

This product is made of FSC®-certified and other controlled material

For Uma + Marlow

# Contents

# Introduction

## From Wisconsin with Love

I grew up on the shores of Lake Michigan, in a small town in Wisconsin near Milwaukee. My universe seemed quite small then, but I always felt a pull to see the world. When I was eight, my mom put my older sister and I on a plane to meet my dad in New York City, where he was already on a work trip. He was there to greet us at LaGuardia and off we went. I remember the trash and the graffiti (it was the 90s!), but I also vividly remember the hotel lobby at the Waldorf Astoria and the cozy, dimly lit booth at 21 Club. The world suddenly opened up for me.

Some twenty-five years later, I would find myself sitting in the Milwaukee airport yet again, this time flying back to my home in NYC. With a celebratory Miller Lite in hand, I nervously typed an email to friends and family announcing the launch of my new wallpaper website. I desperately wanted this dream of mine to flourish. I finished my beer, hit send, and boarded the plane. And so it began.

Now, after more than a decade in business, I still feel like a newcomer in this centuries-old industry. But I find that my fresh perspective has made me a curious and excited student. Wallpaper has always felt like more than just a product to me. It's a window into different eras and memories—an enduring art form that turns walls into stories.

Growing up around my family's printing business, I was surrounded by colors, patterns, and textures that would ultimately become the foundation of my career. When I started Chasing Paper, I wanted to make something accessible and playful that let people write their own design stories. I wanted to build something that people could easily interact with that felt fun and expressive. And what I've come to realize over the years is that wallpaper resonates so deeply because it is a keeper of memories—a reminder of the rooms where life happens.

# Never the Same Old Story

Periods of transformation often punctuate our lives with moments of deep shifting and growing, and wallpaper can be an outward reflection of those times. It illustrates the evolution of personal style and the shift of perspective that life experiences can have on our tastes—and therefore the spaces in which we dwell. Homes are so much more remarkable when we understand the stories of how they came to be.

Peeling back the layers of the past, one finds the joy and heartbreak of people's stories in the thoughtful and intentional creation of their home environments. Each layer of wallpaper creates a tactile history that we can touch and see and feel. Over the years, I've come to appreciate how wallpaper holds this delicate line between permanence and change. It's there for as long as we want it to be, but it's always ready to evolve, to allow a room to take on new energy and meaning.

One of the most magical things about wallpaper is that it can be both nostalgic and entirely fresh. I've seen customers fall in love with a floral pattern that takes them back to their childhood home or a geometric print that creates an entirely different aesthetic in their space. They create new memories and new spaces, even within the comfort of the familiar. This connection between past and present is what makes wallpaper so transformational—and why I felt compelled to highlight that in this book.

# A Love Letter to Wallpaper

In these pages, we'll dive into the evolution of wallpaper, exploring its rich history as well as the innovative leaps that have brought us to the vibrant, varied designs of today. We'll also hear stories of people who have used wallpaper in their projects and the meaning behind their selections.

This book is a celebration of wallpaper's legacy and the powerful nostalgia it elicits. Each print and pattern connects us to memories, blending a whisper of history with the thrill of transformation. It's been a true joy to witness people using our wallpaper to make spaces their own—to reclaim old styles or boldly try new ones, all while creating something uniquely personal.

This job has also allowed me the opportunity to marvel at the creative minds we have had the pleasure of partnering with. From a rockstar-turned-designer to a self-taught DIY darling, our collaborators have been nothing short of inspiring. The second half of this book will give you a glimpse into the background of some of the creatives in this community and illustrate how they translated their own inspiration into works of art for our walls.

So let's step into this world together. Let's embrace the nostalgia, celebrate the creativity, and honor the way wallpaper has accompanied us through history, bringing joy, elegance, and expression into our lives. Here's to wallpaper: to its enduring beauty, its storytelling magic, and the countless ways it inspires us to make every room a place worth remembering.

# PART 1

# Nostalgia

Wallpaper is not just a quick decorating fix. Most people take time to really consider their wall-covering options before taking the plunge. And for good reason! Wallpaper often becomes a foundational element in a space and the thing people remember most about it.

This section will show scenes from some of my most vivid memories and how I paid tribute to them when designing my own spaces. But first, a short history lesson.

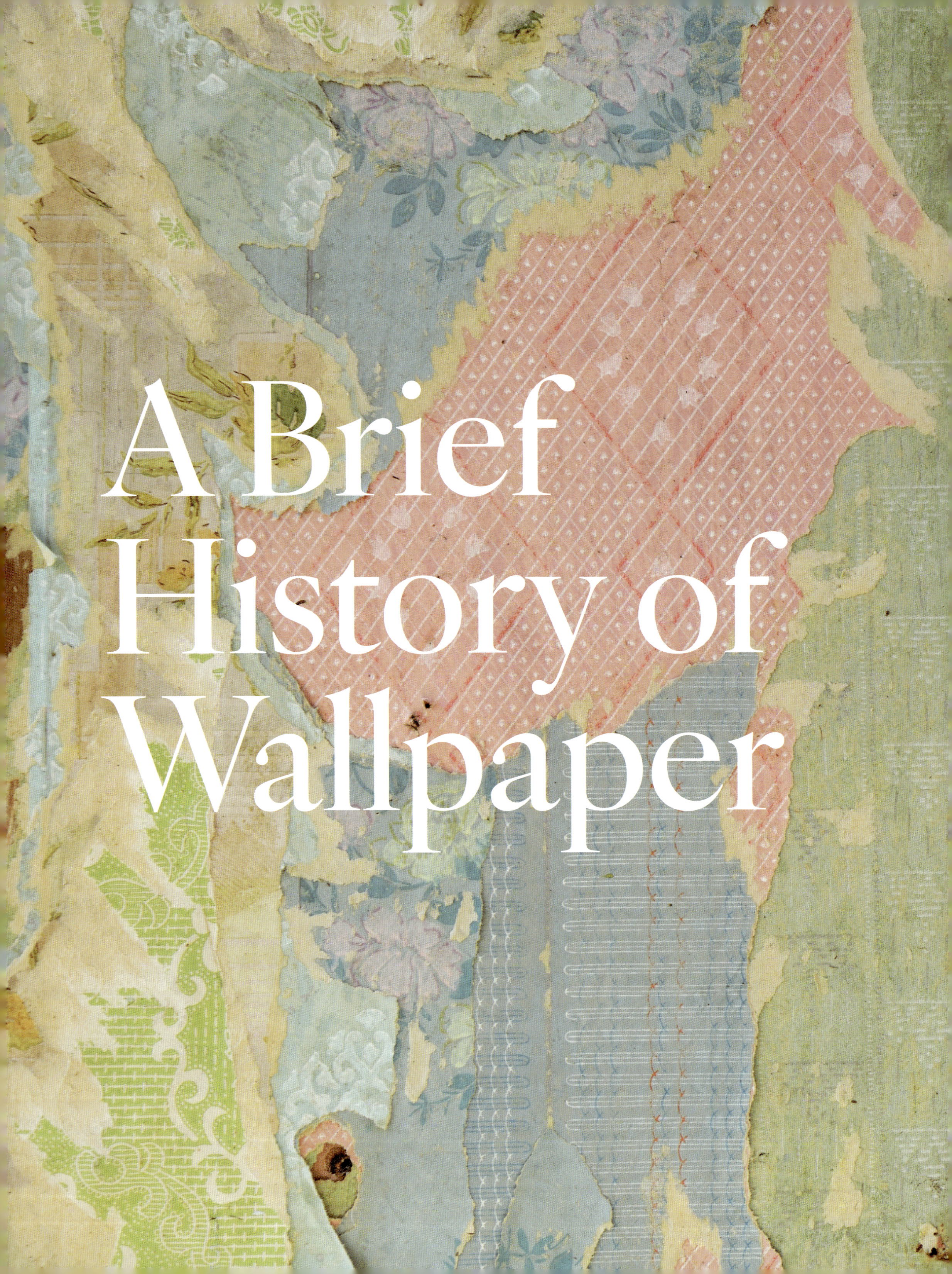
A Brief
History of
Wallpaper

Wallpaper has such a rich, layered past. From *trompe l'oeil* designs used to trick the eye to artful patterns meant to show off personal style, wallpaper can make spaces feel personal, warm, and expressive. Here's a look back through some defining moments in wallpaper history.

**EARLY DAYS:** In the mid-1500s, the European elite started using painted cloths to decorate their walls. Back then, wall hangings were more like painted sheets of paper pinned to walls—a cheaper substitute to expensive tapestries. The first wallpapers were block printed, sometimes even hand painted, with rich patterns that mimicked textiles. As trade routes expanded, so did the wallpaper market. With the arrival of Chinese and Japanese papermaking techniques, Europe experienced a wallpaper boom. The French were particularly taken with intricate designs and *chinoiserie* (Chinese-inspired art) was everywhere. Skilled craftsmen created papers that told stories of exotic lands, flora, and fauna. The patterns were evolving, and wallpaper started to reflect personal taste and sophistication.

**221 BC** Wallpaper likely originated in China during the Qin dynasty.

**1634** Flock wallpapers are designed to look like cut velvet but, in fact, are made using powdered wool, which would otherwise go to waste.

**1509** The earliest known wallpaper in Britain emerges. After this, wallpaper sheets measure about eleven by fourteen inches and are often used to line chests or boxes. Multiple sheets are sometimes pasted on canvas before being nailed up as a wall covering.

**1675** Frenchman Jean-Michel Papillon creates the first repeating designs that match on both ends of the sheet, allowing for sheets to be connected into rolls.

**Late 1600s** Chinese hand-painted wallpapers are imported to Europe and become increasingly popular. So much so that it prompts the production of European imitations.

**Early 1700s** Thanks to the introduction of continuous rolls, large-scale repeats are now possible.

**1712** Noticing an increase in demand for wallpaper, Queen Anne imposes a tax on the product that lasts for 124 years.

**1765** The first wallpaper factory in America opens.

**INDUSTRIAL REVOLUTION AND MASS PRODUCTION:** The industrial age changed everything. Suddenly, wallpaper could be produced much faster and more affordably, making it accessible to more than just the aristocracy. The rise of machine-printed patterns meant that everyone could add a personal touch to their homes. The Victorians went wild for bold, dark colors and heavy patterns, filling every inch with drama.

**Early 1800s**
Whole-wall murals are introduced.

**1841** The first machine-printed designs are sold.

**1839** A machine is invented that can produce about 400 rolls per day and print with four colors (by 1874, up to twenty colors can be used). After this machine's invention, wallpaper production jumped from a reported 1.2 million rolls per year (1834) to 32 million rolls in 1874.

**1861** William Morris of Morris, Marshall, Faulkner & Co. (now Morris & Co.) fought against the mechanization of the printing process and created hand-drawn, hand-carved designs that remain popular to this day.

### Weird Wallpaper Fact

Arsenic was commonly used in the production of wallpaper and other decorating products. By the 1870s, it was determined that the vapor produced by damp wallpapers, paints, and fabric could lead to illness or even death. Oil-based pigments were used after that.

**1888** Ferdinand Sichel invents wallpaper paste.

**1889** F. Schumacher and Co., a heritage brand still in existence today, is founded.

Decoration, designed by Mr. Louis C. Tiffany.

**1898** Gracie Studio, renowned for their hand-painted wall coverings, is founded.

**ART DECO, MODERNISM, AND POST-WAR PATTERNS:** In the early 1900s, art deco brought glamour and geometric patterns to the world of wallpaper. But by the mid-twentieth century, modernism called for simplicity, and many people embraced minimalist, solid-colored walls, leading to a bit of a wallpaper lull. Then the 1960s and '70s reignited wallpaper fever with vibrant, retro designs in bright hues and funky shapes. By the '80s, wallpaper in homes ranged from floral prints to pastels and soft geometrics as design tastes grew even more diverse.

**1904** The Arts & Crafts movement incorporates nature-inspired motifs in organic colors.

**1920s** Considered the "Golden Age of Wallpaper," this decade is known for celebrating the gilded and geometric designs of the art deco era.

**1930s** More subdued colors and styles enter during the Great Depression.

**1933** American heritage textile and wall-covering brand Sister Parish is founded. It is currently a fourth-generation, female-owned company.

**1940s** During World War II, wallpaper designs become simple and restrained.

**1950s** This post-war period introduces the "Good Design" movement of flat, linear patterns and symbols of the Atomic Era.

**1960s** Bold color and geometric designs are prevalent in everything from textiles to wallpaper.

**1961** Pre-pasted and trimmed papers first appear, soon followed by washable vinyl.

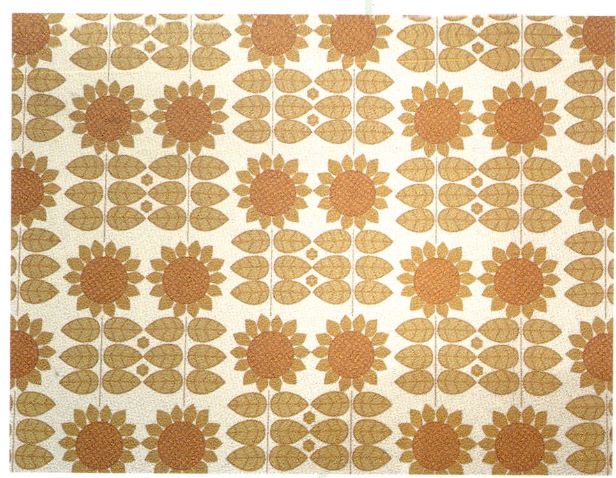

**1970s** Large-scale florals and geometrics in bright earthy tones are popularized. Flocked finishes make a comeback.

**1973** There is a worldwide reduction of wallpaper production due to the oil crisis.

**1980s** Neon shades and graphic shapes highlight the statement-making excess of the era.

**1990s** Styles shift to a more subdued and neutral palette featuring plenty of stripes and faux finishes.

**A RESURGENCE IN PATTERN AND SELF-EXPRESSION:** The past two decades have been transformative. Wallpaper is no longer just about covering walls; it's about self-expression and transforming spaces in ways that paint alone can't do. Peel-and-stick technology has opened up the world of wallpaper to everyone, making it a playful, easy, and commitment-free way to style a space. Whether it's a full wall or an accent panel, wallpaper today is about telling a story and bringing joy into the home.

**May 2020** New panel sizes are added to the Chasing Paper website.

**1993** The era of digital printing begins.

**1997** Self-adhesive wall coverings are created.

**2000s** The term "eclectic" seems the best way to describe the vast array of wallpaper options. Accent walls are popularized.

**2013** Chasing Paper launches with a single product: two-by-four-foot peel-and-stick panels.

**June 2020** Chasing Paper launches traditional, nonwoven options.

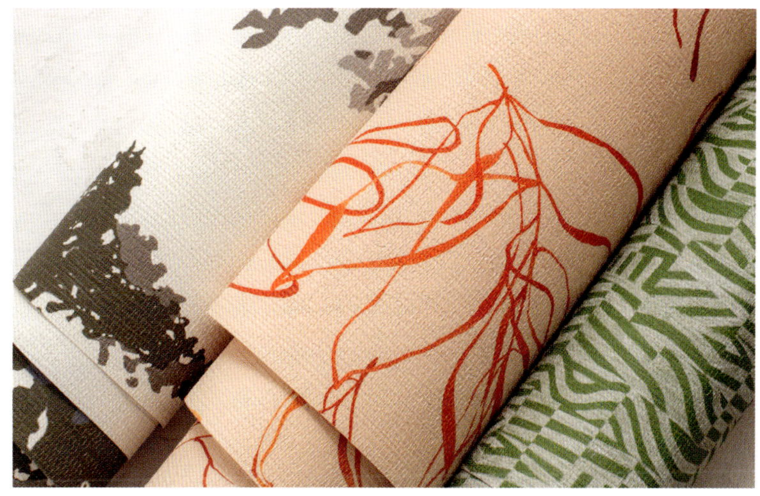

**February 2023** Faux grasscloth is added to the Chasing Paper website.

**June 2023** Chasing Paper adds matte vinyl to their offerings.

**September 2021** Elizabeth and Chasing Paper are featured in *Better Homes & Gardens*.

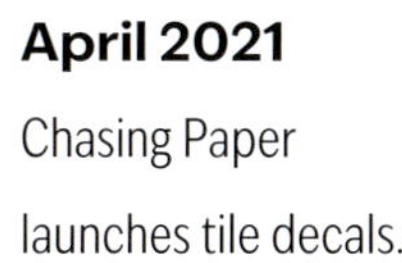

**April 2021** Chasing Paper launches tile decals.

# It's All Relative

Working with family is a unique kind of magic—it's equal parts challenging and rewarding. My brother Mike has been such a fundamental part of Chasing Paper's journey, and I wouldn't have it any other way. When we first started this adventure, we had no idea how intertwined our lives and skills would become, but it's been such a gift to grow alongside him, not just as siblings but as collaborators.

What's special about working with my brother is the shorthand we share. There's a deep trust that comes from growing up together—those long car rides, shared holidays, and a lifetime of inside jokes translate into an unspoken understanding in the workplace.

One of my favorite things about working together is seeing how our strengths complement each other. Where I dive headfirst into creativity and big-picture ideas, he brings a practicality and precision that keeps everything balanced.

At the end of the day, working with family is about connection. It's about pouring our shared values into something bigger than ourselves and building a legacy that's rooted in love, respect, and creating something our kids would be proud of.

ALLEGRA HICKS
WONDERLAND

We are always looking for a fresh perspective, a fresh idea, something that we haven't seen a million times over, or a new way of looking at a pattern. It's actually pretty rare that we see something truly unique.

Right before we launched our tile collection, I felt a surge of inspiration from a recent trip to Portugal. The tile work we saw there stirred up a new creative vision for our team.

We don't reverse engineer collections trying to fill a gap in our lineup. We identify collaborators who we believe have a unique idea and help them bring that to life.

When I was first starting out and living in New York, I wanted a product that really felt like I could do it myself. We started with two-by-four-foot panels because the size felt manageable for a single person to handle. The small scale also allowed customers to get creative—using the paper not only on their walls but also on their cabinets, refrigerators, and old furniture.

We shoot everything in natural light to create this aspirational moment versus simply photoshopping (the standard industry method).

CA
VA
BIEN!

In our sampling process, we can play with scale and colorways, print it, and see each pattern in real life before making additional tweaks.

We print digitally on-demand, which, in the wallpaper world, some people think is really cool and technologically advanced, while other people are against because they view hand painting or block printing to be the only appropriate methods. But digital allows us to remain affordable and responsive.

Since starting Chasing Paper in 2013, my eyes have been opened to a world of pattern and design. And most importantly, the fact that there are people behind all the wallpaper we see: the artists who created the design, the grandmother who picked it out for her home, the child who stares up at their nursery wallpaper. This keeps us inspired to create wallpaper that will lead to lasting memories.

**Mike Rees**
**Milwaukee, WI**

# Lalla's Legacy

**Margaret Rees**
**Wilmette, IL**

Meet my grandmother, Margaret ("Lalla" to everyone who knows her). She is the kind of person whose presence fills a room—not just because she has a natural elegance about her, but because she carries herself with such purpose and care. Growing up, I was endlessly inspired by her love of beautiful things: the way she picked out an outfit, her knack for setting a table that felt both grand and inviting, and, of course, her unmatched appreciation for pattern and design.

Lalla has this gift for making spaces feel alive. Her home isn't just a place where we gathered as a family, it is a reflection of her heart and the experiences of her life. The wallpapers she chose, the textiles she layered, the color palettes—it all tells a story. And as a little girl, I was captivated. I'd run my fingers across her wallpapered walls, tracing the lines of intricate florals and geometric patterns, marveling at how something so simple could transform a space into something magical. I would sleep among the blue wallpapered walls with my sisters close by, feeling enveloped in another world.

Our shared love for design became a bond that deepened as I grew older. When I would come home from New York for holidays, she would have stacks of magazines for me and my sisters—pages marked with spaces or ideas she found interesting.

More than anything, my grandmother taught me that design, like family, is about layers. Decades of stories and experiences create the fabric of our family.

Recently, I asked Lalla about her personal relationship with wallpaper and if she had any specific memories of it growing up. She recalled when her mother hired a decorator, and they selected a beautiful light-green damask wallpaper for the living room. Before installing it, Lalla and her siblings signed their names on the wall. Decades later, the new owner of that house recognized Lalla. They told her that they had uncovered the signatures as they were redecorating and invited her to come see them. Those are the treasures these houses hold as you peel back the layers.

"I don't like a lot of different patterns but if I do have different patterns, I don't want them to clash."

After my grandmother was married, her younger sister was in college and working at a wallpaper store during the summer. "She was always very artistic, and I admired that. I wanted to wallpaper the bathroom in our home, and we decided to do the whole space—including the ceiling. It was not very big, but the two of us could hardly get the paste up *and* hold the paper. We finally finished, but I would never do it again." Lalla was ahead of the curve with so many things. Papering all four walls and the ceiling is a go-to choice of designers these days.

**Left:** A vignette of some of Lalla's most special moments and the ones we shared.

**Above:** The guest room in Lalla's home is a perfect balance of feminine touch and nostalgia.

Now that I've run Chasing Paper for over a decade, I look at my grandmother's home with new eyes and realize what an impact it had on me. Subconsciously, I mimicked her design style (left) a bit in our lake house design (right). Pattern on pattern in a way that makes my heart (and hers) happy!

# Manifestation of Memories

**Elizabeth's home**
**Milwaukee, WI**

After admiring my grandmother's home for decades, I was finally able to put my stamp on the Milwaukee home I share with my husband and our two daughters.

This paper is called Kent Street from our Heritage Collection. Kent Street is the street my brother and I grew up on and this print has foundations of traditional design with a little bit of modern quirk added in. I want the places where we're spending family time to feel as complete as possible. This breakfast nook will be the backdrop to so many of my girls' memories.

I left this room stark white for years—and it's the room you walk into when you first enter my house! But I wanted it to include something that came out of my own brain. After ten years of Chasing Paper, I felt strongly about creating a print myself and this is the result. This is my personality in room form.

**Right:** We chose to juxtapose traditional motifs in my daughters' rooms (plaid in Uma's and toile in Marlow's) with modern accessories and art.

**Below:** The green nursery is my daughter Marlow's room. It was the first room in the house that we completed. The house was built in 1912 and the board and batten was screaming for wallpaper above—and our tree toile fit the bill perfectly.

*Kids' rooms are the gateway to wallpaper for many people.*

**Above:** The Samara print in our primary bedroom is a watercolor design that, from far away, almost looks textural. Playing with patterns can seem daunting, but it's also a fun way to individualize your space. Stick to two or three complementary patterns per room to avoid visual chaos and pair large, bold prints with smaller, more intricate patterns to create contrast without overwhelming the space.

Consider wallpapering the back of a hutch, using wallpaper as a mat within a frame, or covering the angled walls surrounding dormered windows to highlight the architectural detail. I've even seen clients use our peel-and-stick wallpaper to transform the look of a refrigerator—there are practically no limits!

**Left:** The print we chose for our dining room is a bit of an homage to my grandmother, who used to put doilies under everything. It's subtle, but the edge of the stripe mimics the lacy edge of a doily. The burgundy is a traditional color but is made to feel modern here through the addition of burnt-orange accents.

**Above:** This is our basement bar and the wallpaper behind the shelving is our New York print. It features images of some iconic NYC restaurants and is a nod to where my husband and I first met. The placement here is also a nod to the early days of Chasing Paper because so many people used our products to accent small spaces like this.

**Above:** This is our sweet pup Rudi modeling atop our peel-and-stick floor tiles, if you can believe it.

**Right:** Adjacent to the bar, we made this flex space for our girls. We chose a fun woodland print in the peel-and-stick style because I know their tastes will evolve as they age, and I want this space to grow with them.

We treated our bathrooms like a boutique hotel, where each one feels different and full of unexpected character.

**Left:** Curves help to offset the sharp angles of the roofline here—even down to the cabinet hardware.

**Center:** Blue tones and warm wood are a classic combo, while the brass accents brighten things up.

**Right:** Small spaces are some of my favorite spots to wallpaper. This cheery Dot Comb print is bold but doesn't overpower the room.

# Life at the Lake

**Elizabeth's Lake House**
**West Bend, WI**

While our lake house was built in the 1970s, we went with an even more retro vibe in the kitchen with bright butter yellow cabinets and warm accents. We aimed to make things light and bright to keep the focus on the view out to the water.

**Opposite:** There is such a richness that comes from layering patterns and textures. The scalloped stripes and botanical prints pair perfectly while the jute and woven elements instantly warm everything up.

**Above:** If you look in the mirror, you'll see a peek at the floral print we used in the adjoining bedroom. Mixing patterns can feel intimidating, but the aim should always be complementary but still unexpected.

**Above:** This Porto wallpaper gives the look of tile without the labor and expense.

**Opposite:** Our dining room is my favorite room of the house—the intersection of casual and chintz

The basement is where you access the house from the lake, so it made sense for that to become our family hang out spot.

The kitchenette down here means we don't have to schlep up and down the stairs when entertaining. It has quickly become the most-used spot in the home.

**Right:** Most of the bathrooms at the lake house were additions, but we opted for finishes with tons of patina to make each feel like it has always been there.

**Opposite:** For the girls' bunk room, we wanted something that felt fun and nostalgic and the Patchwork print from Max Humphrey's collection fit the bill perfectly.

**Right:** I took a page from Lalla's design book in this space with tons of layered patterns. Since this part of the house doesn't get a lot of natural light, we went with our Market Floral print on the walls and ceiling to create an ultra-cozy cocooning effect.

**Following:** The beautiful layers of my family. I love to revisit old photos and see that I have always been surrounded by lots of pattern and a whole lot of love.

# PART 2

# In Conversation

When I sat down to write this book, I knew I wanted it to be more than just a collection of beautiful rooms. Design, at its core, is about people—how we live, what we love, and the stories our spaces tell. That's why, when it came time to choose the designers featured in this section, I didn't have to look too far. Each artist represents a personal connection and a partnership built over years of collaboration, creativity, and trust.

Design is never created in a vacuum. It's shaped by conversations, connections, and the shared sparks of inspiration that come from working alongside others. I invite you into the creative worlds of nine designers who have not only used wallpaper as a vehicle for inspired design, but have also profoundly influenced my journey with Chasing Paper. Some of these designers were among the first to believe in Chasing Paper, incorporating our wallpaper into their work in ways that were fresh, unexpected, and entirely their own. Others are longtime friends—people I've admired for their ability to transform a space with an effortless mix of form and feeling.

These friends and collaborators each bring a distinct vision to their craft, reflecting the unique stories, places, and passions that drive their work. As you turn the pages, you'll see their artistry come to life, and you'll get to know the people behind the patterns—in their own voices. These are the dreamers who reimagine walls as canvases, transforming spaces into places of joy, comfort, and expression. Their stories remind us that great design is more than a product—it's a conversation that continues to evolve.

# Max Humphrey

SPORTSMASTER

**Max Humphrey**
**Portland, OR**

# Meet Max

**MAX HUMPHREY** *was born in western New Hampshire and had a pretty idyllic boyhood: running in the woods, lighting things on fire, and shooting at (and missing) squirrels. That all changed when the first Nintendo console was released. After that, for every day spent outdoors in the summer, Max needed a full day inside playing Super Mario Brothers—and he says that's stuck with him into adulthood. In his early twenties, Max lived the life of a rock star for a few years, traveling the world to play shows. When the band broke up, he landed in LA and started looking for work. Ultimately, he fell into the career of interior design with a side hustle as a product designer. Max's storied past has given him inspiration to create meaningful designs that have clients and collaborators alike seeking his expertise.*

## HOW WE MET

Max and I began our friendship—like so many these days—on the internet. We liked each other's posts, commented cheerfully with emojis, and eventually started messaging and kicking around the idea of a collaboration. Before Max, working with an interior designer had not been something we were well acquainted with at Chasing Paper. Still, the idea excited us both. Interior designers understand what wallpaper is available on the market, what prints are overused, and what designs they search for and, often, cannot find. We began the process of building a collection and soon found that there was something impossibly exciting brewing.

Modern Americana
Stay Gold
CRAFTSBURY GENERAL STORE
BIRDS in Our Lives
Balance of rustic with modern elements

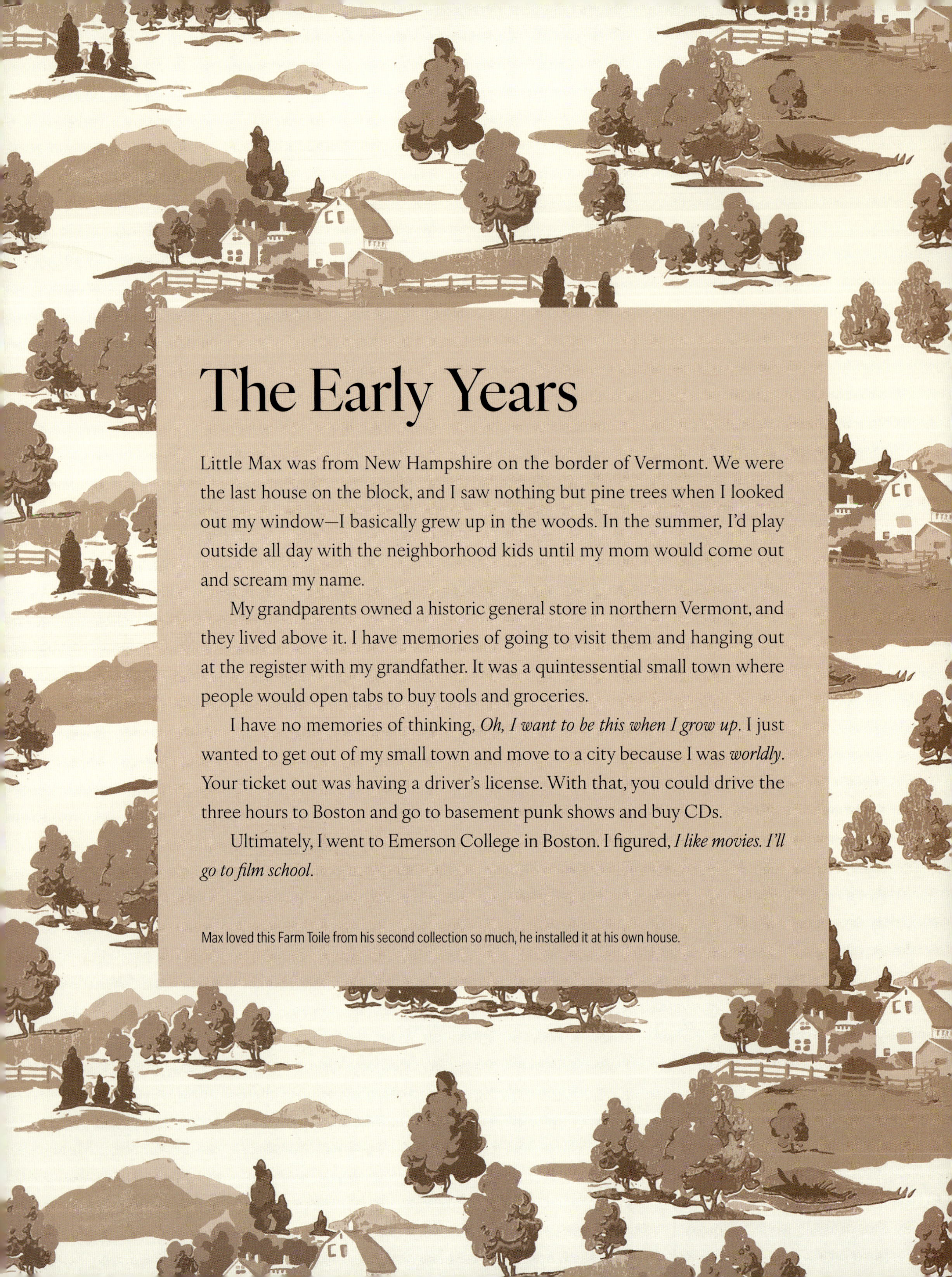

# The Early Years

Little Max was from New Hampshire on the border of Vermont. We were the last house on the block, and I saw nothing but pine trees when I looked out my window—I basically grew up in the woods. In the summer, I'd play outside all day with the neighborhood kids until my mom would come out and scream my name.

My grandparents owned a historic general store in northern Vermont, and they lived above it. I have memories of going to visit them and hanging out at the register with my grandfather. It was a quintessential small town where people would open tabs to buy tools and groceries.

I have no memories of thinking, *Oh, I want to be this when I grow up*. I just wanted to get out of my small town and move to a city because I was *worldly*. Your ticket out was having a driver's license. With that, you could drive the three hours to Boston and go to basement punk shows and buy CDs.

Ultimately, I went to Emerson College in Boston. I figured, *I like movies. I'll go to film school.*

Max loved this Farm Toile from his second collection so much, he installed it at his own house.

FRIENDSHIP IS A
SHELTERING
TREE
TRUE NORTH

MODERN
AMERICANA
Coleman

# Cultivating Creativity

After film school, I moved to LA and worked in the TV and film industry, photocopying scripts and making coffee runs. A few years in, I was playing in a punk band, and we were offered a record deal with a major indie label. We got to quit our jobs, make a record, and go on tour. We were on the road for two years straight, staying in motels all across the US and Europe. When we got back to LA, the band broke up and I had to reenter society. I had always lived with a dozen roommates, so I opted to try it solo this time around. I rented my first apartment in the basement of a 1920s hotel-turned-apartment building. I was unemployed, but I needed stuff and I needed color. I'd go to thrift stores, paint (and repaint) the walls, then have people come over and watch how they reacted to my apartment. I really fed off of that feedback. So it got me thinking: *What's the job version of picking out paint colors and rearranging furniture?* I had never heard the term "interior design," so I went to bookstores and the library to try to figure it out. Then I realized there was this whole industry out there.

I learned that there was a trend in the '50s and '60s for movie set decorators to transition into interior design and that made sense to me. So I found a job listing on Craigslist for a part-time design assistant at a boutique interior design firm. I didn't have any practical skills, but I was very competent and self-aware. My boss was like, "Oh, you can't do the drawings, so you might as well come to the client meeting and carry the binders." Because of that, I was in front of clients very early on and I stuck around until I moved to Portland to start my own firm.

A beautiful botanical print that almost feels tongue-in-cheek when you realize what type of plant it is (poison ivy!).

# Childhood Home

When I was a teenager, I started going to punk shows in southern New Hampshire, Boston, and even New York and saw how they would wheatpaste posters all over the walls. Then I would go back to my bedroom and realize my walls were super blank. I couldn't afford to buy artwork, so I'd plaster posters on the walls instead. These posters felt very meaningful and offered a way to connect with other people and start a conversation.

It's only recently that I've been able to remember what my childhood home looked like. I didn't clock that as a kid. I have to look at pictures because I just wasn't interested in it back then. My parents liked to go antique shopping, and they'd drag me and my little sister to these country antique malls. As a ten-year-old boy, it felt like the worst way to spend a Saturday. It's ironic, because now that's my favorite thing to do.

Looking back at pictures of my house growing up, I realize that the patterns I've been creating were there. When I did my quilt wallpaper with Chasing Paper, my mom pointed out that we had quilts all over our house in gingham, buffalo check, and ticking stripe. I didn't replicate those intentionally.

What goes around comes around. Max breathed new life into classic patterns for his first wallpaper collection.

KEYSTONE
SORRY!
MONOPOLY

# Creating a Collection

I'm inspired by vintage, so I want everything to be kind of vintagey or handmade looking. My ginghams, for example, have texture and the lines aren't razor sharp. Even though it's new and contemporary, it's supposed to look like it's always been there. And that's the same with all the patterns. They could be simple from far away, but if you get up close, there's an organic nature to them. And the color palette has always been about bringing the outdoors in.

You know how sometimes you see fashion shows with really maximalist clothing and then the fashion designer comes out in a black T-shirt and black pants? That's always seemed so bizarre to me. When I'm designing, I'm only designing for myself. If I haven't used one of my patterns in one of my own projects, it's a failure. And it probably reflects in the sales numbers, too. I'm my best client so that's who I'm designing for.

Design is very similar to songwriting. If you try and write a hit song, it never happens. But the one that pops into your head in the shower? That's a win.

Max says he's partial to big patterns that make a statement and that's just what his designs do.

"Design is very similar to songwriting. If you try and write a hit song, it never happens. But the one that pops into your head in the shower? That's a win."

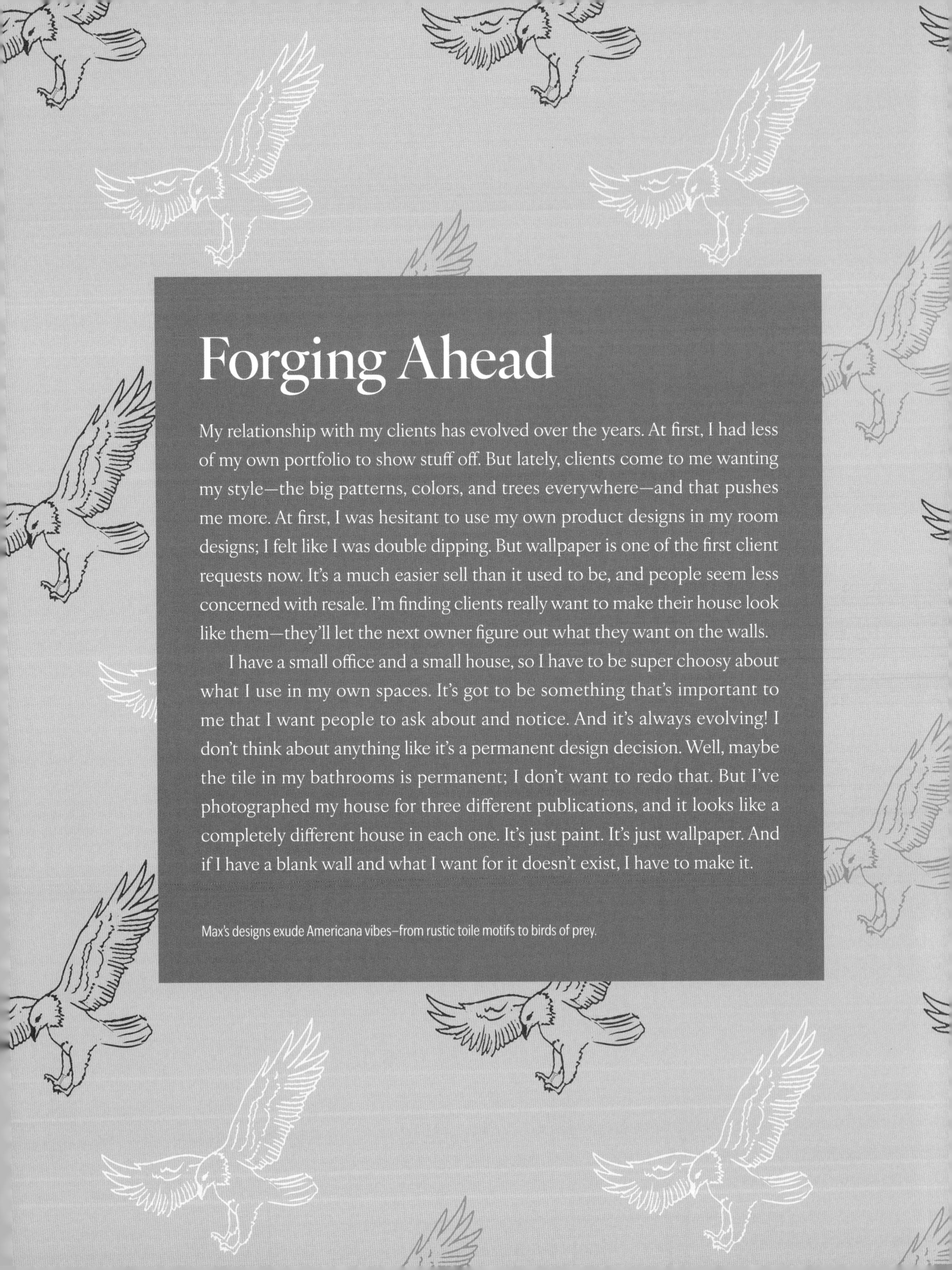

# Forging Ahead

My relationship with my clients has evolved over the years. At first, I had less of my own portfolio to show stuff off. But lately, clients come to me wanting my style—the big patterns, colors, and trees everywhere—and that pushes me more. At first, I was hesitant to use my own product designs in my room designs; I felt like I was double dipping. But wallpaper is one of the first client requests now. It's a much easier sell than it used to be, and people seem less concerned with resale. I'm finding clients really want to make their house look like them—they'll let the next owner figure out what they want on the walls.

I have a small office and a small house, so I have to be super choosy about what I use in my own spaces. It's got to be something that's important to me that I want people to ask about and notice. And it's always evolving! I don't think about anything like it's a permanent design decision. Well, maybe the tile in my bathrooms is permanent; I don't want to redo that. But I've photographed my house for three different publications, and it looks like a completely different house in each one. It's just paint. It's just wallpaper. And if I have a blank wall and what I want for it doesn't exist, I have to make it.

Max's designs exude Americana vibes—from rustic toile motifs to birds of prey.

Jenni
Yolo

**Jenni Yolo**
**Milwaukee, WI**

# Meet Jenni

*A natural born creative,* **JENNI YOLO** *honed her DIY skills early on, testing techniques for tie-dye or friendship bracelets and upcycling clothing. Before starting the wildly popular do-it-yourself website I Spy DIY, Jenni worked in the magazine industry in New York City. After hours, she would recreate runway styles on a budget and her creations caught the eye of an editor at* InStyle *magazine. From there, a brand was born. This big break led Jenni to move back to her home state of Wisconsin and run I Spy DIY full time, where she began to focus more on home content than fashion. While she and her husband are renovating old homes in their area, they are also filming a TV show called* Makeover by Monday.

**HOW WE MET**

As I was plotting my exit out of NYC, my publicist emailed me about an influencer from Milwaukee. I was immediately curious about this wildly creative woman from my hometown. Jenni and I eventually met for dinner, and I was struck by her sheer creative force. Her ability to make big ideas and renovations seem relatable and accessible to a large audience was awe-inspiring. Jenni has such a strong tie to the past and infuses so much life into new spaces using vintage treasures. She used that same influence when creating her wallpaper collection with us, bringing historical references and images to our meetings. Afterward, it was incredible to see how she designed (and continues to design) spaces around that.

Cosmos remind me of my girls.

Looking at that kid photo, I realized that the wallpaper designs I create now resemble those from my childhood home. Maybe fewer hens . . . but in essence—the stripes and florals—are still there! A sweet little reminder that some designs hold a timeless charm.

# Where It All Began

I grew up in Manitowoc, Wisconsin. My parents tell me that they saw my creativity as a kid, and they let me do what I wanted. I would jump from thing to thing: drum lessons then sewing classes. There was a park down the street where they would often host crafting sessions. One day it might be tie-dye, so I'd run home and grab the sheets from my bed and my siblings' beds and come home with a "Surprise!" That park was a great place where I was able to test out different mediums, which ended up being the building blocks for the DIY projects I'd do later in life. Whenever I became interested in something, I became all-consumed with it. That's how I am with my business now.

The Dahlia print from Jenni's wallpaper collection exudes freshness and the new possibilities of springtime.

# The Path Forward

When I was probably 12 years old, I had gotten my own room and I covered my walls and ceiling with ripped pages from magazines, the Delia catalog, and CD covers. It was my first version of wallpaper. I liked the idea of having stuff on the walls that immediately shared what I was into. It was a great way to self-express.

I think those pasted pages started this whole idea that I wanted to work in magazines. I found a note I wrote when I was young that said, "I want to move to New York City and work in advertising." I don't think I really knew what that meant other than that it was a job I knew you could be creative in. Ultimately, I studied magazine design, moved to New York, and started working at *InStyle* magazine doing page layout and design.

While working at the magazine, I was seeing all of these clothing designs that we were featuring and I remember thinking, *I can't afford the designer version of this*. So, out of necessity, I started making DIY versions. Michael Kors and grommet embellishments were really popular then, so I recreated something with grommets for myself, and an editor saw it and asked if I could make more. So, of course, I went home and whipped up a dozen different DIY designer-inspired outfits and accessories, which turned into a story for the September issue of *InStyle*. Before it went to print, they asked me if I had a website. I did not, so I started I Spy DIY. And that is what catapulted my whole career.

I realize now that I was able to turn the piecing things together and experimenting I was doing as a kid into a job where I was piecing things together on a page. Ultimately, I think that really helped with how I design, too, because whenever I look at a room, I'm almost looking at it as a picture: I'm piecing things together and composing what I think a beautiful photo would be.

The Lace print adds a touch of whimsy and delight to any space.

# Time for Transition

Ultimately, I got priced out of New York. I was visiting my sisters in Milwaukee and they said, "Let's just go look at warehouse spaces here." I heard the price and, three months later, moved to Wisconsin and into that space. That's where I switched from doing DIY fashion to more DIY home stuff. In the Midwest, home content was more relatable than fashion.

I bought my first reno house for $24,000 and fixed it up in four months for a pilot for HGTV. I didn't know what I was doing, and I painted everything white. I lived in it for a bit and realized it was lacking character and interest. It was around this time that I discovered Chasing Paper, and the idea of peel-and-stick wallpaper offered so much freedom. I could easily change it if I wanted to. And I did! I started with a green floral pattern in my bathroom and switched it out for the more organic and leafy Botany wallpaper that has now been up for years. It blew people's minds to see that room in two totally different lights and to realize how simple it was to do.

I recommend this to people who are renovating: just paint the whole thing white. Live with it. See how you use it. Then start incorporating color and pattern.

Jenni installed the tonal Cosmos Block Print in her kitchen to provide subtle pattern that can still be layered on top of with other artwork and accessories.

# Finding Inspiration

I was born and grew up in the same house, and it was covered in wallpaper. Then in the mid-90s, my parents renovated and took it all out. Some of the original wallpaper was tacky, so I wasn't sad it came down, but the all-beige result felt too extreme. It felt like the house lost its character. I actually think that's when I started finding my design style. I decided to be more adventurous with my room design. I think I was trying to add flavor into our house that had become very vanilla.

After I had the opportunity to design a wallpaper collection with Chasing Paper, I realized that I unconsciously created styles that were reminiscent of those in my house growing up. Turns out that the wallpapers that have the most meaning to me are the ones that sell the best.

Ticking Tulip has become a best-selling staple that so many of our customers confidently add to their homes. It feels timeless and adds texture and warmth. We love that Jenni added it to her own home too.

RURAL ESCAPES
RURAL ESCAPES
THOMAS O'BRIEN
A PLACE TO CALL HOME GIL SCHAFER III

WC

# A Sign from the Cosmos

I love cosmos flowers and, by proxy, my daughter does too. They are wild and resilient little blooms that seem to pop up everywhere. And I think that's what I am: a resilient roadside flower that won't go away—a little bit wild. I wanted to translate that into a wallpaper.

When I was pregnant with my second, my daughter and I planted cosmos seeds in the yard. When I came home from the hospital, there were two cosmos blooming there—one for each of my girls. So I used the Cosmos paper when we designed their shared bedroom. I also used it in my kitchen. Now this meaningful design will be in the backdrop of so many of my daughters' memories as they grow up.

There are so many wallpaper options out there and you don't really know the story behind each. That's the beauty of the internet: I can share my stories and give insight into each pattern's meaning. I think people find their own personal connection to a design that way.

This image set the internet on fire and Cosmo quickly became the best-selling pattern for Chasing Paper.

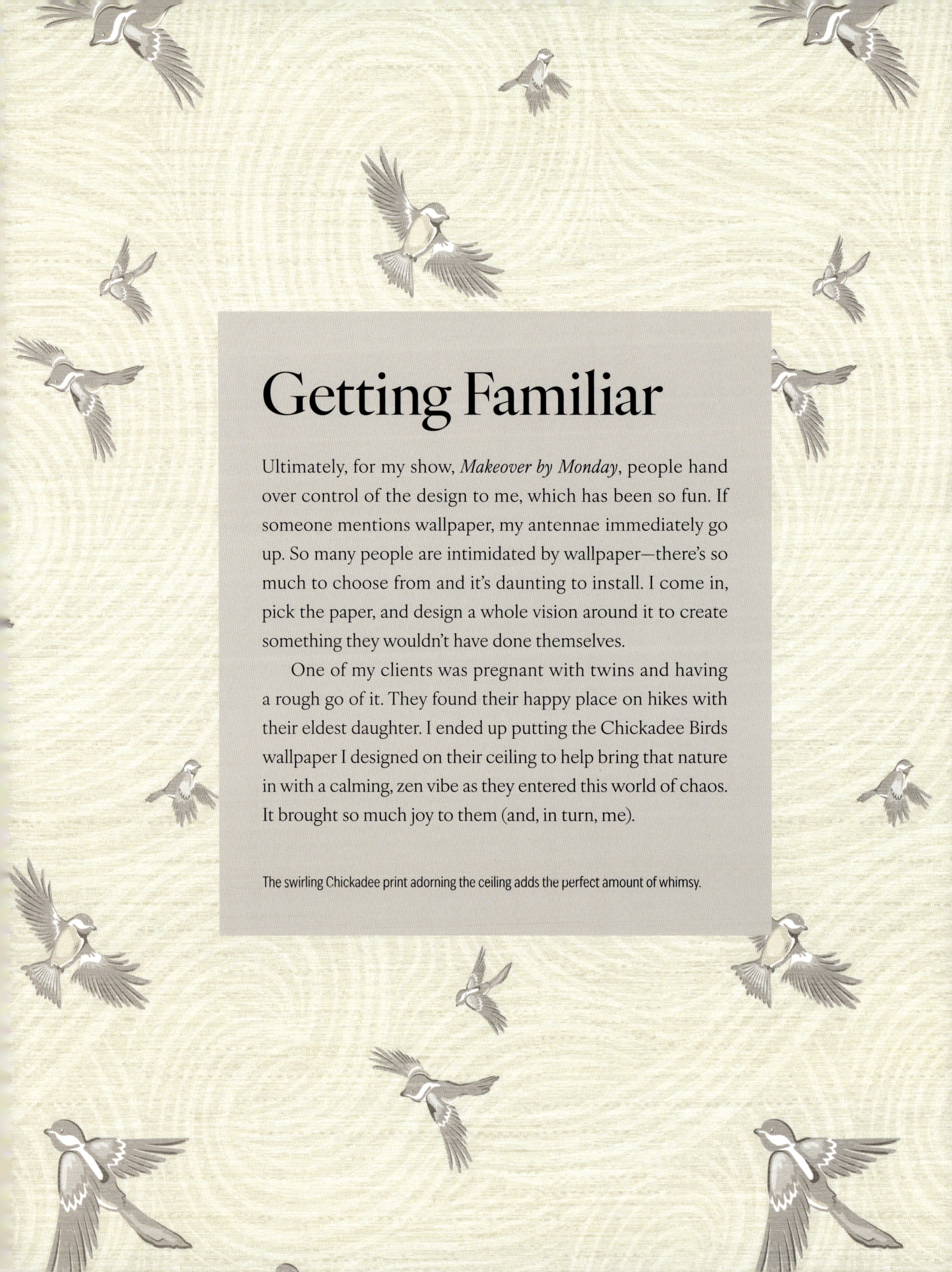

# Getting Familiar

Ultimately, for my show, *Makeover by Monday*, people hand over control of the design to me, which has been so fun. If someone mentions wallpaper, my antennae immediately go up. So many people are intimidated by wallpaper—there's so much to choose from and it's daunting to install. I come in, pick the paper, and design a whole vision around it to create something they wouldn't have done themselves.

One of my clients was pregnant with twins and having a rough go of it. They found their happy place on hikes with their eldest daughter. I ended up putting the Chickadee Birds wallpaper I designed on their ceiling to help bring that nature in with a calming, zen vibe as they entered this world of chaos. It brought so much joy to them (and, in turn, me).

The swirling Chickadee print adorning the ceiling adds the perfect amount of whimsy.

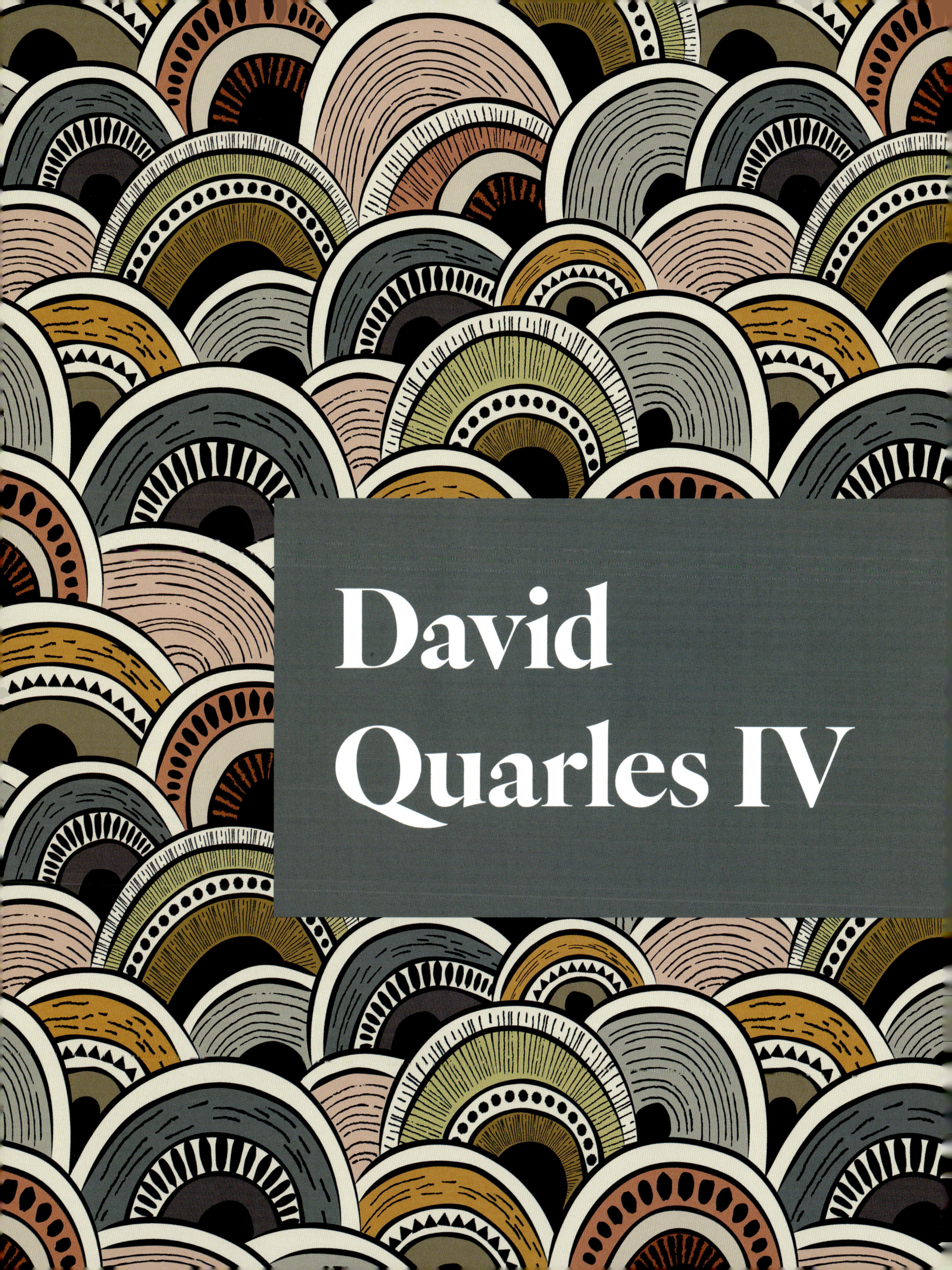
David
Quarles IV

**David Quarles IV**
**Memphis, TN**

# Meet David

*Some people are instantly likeable, and* **DAVID QUARLES IV** *of Memphis certainly is that. He has an infectiously positive outlook and the ability to create luxuriously layered spaces that feel as warm and inviting as he is. Drawing from his family's diverse heritage, David often incorporates relevant pattern, color, and texture into his own spaces—and he does the same for his clients, introducing elements that best represent who they are.*

## HOW WE MET

David is sunshine personified. The first time he and I connected on the phone, I was walking around my front yard. When I hung up, one of my neighbor's said to me, "That must have been a good call. You did not stop smiling the whole time you were talking!" And it was true—my cheeks were sore because David has a way of conjuring happiness and hope in a way that I have experienced very few times in my life. His design style and ability to bring color, print, and pattern into a home is truly unmatched and wallpaper plays such a big part in his story.

Warmth

Create scenes where people can be their happiest.

# The Origin Story

I was inspired by design early on through my grandmother and my dad. My grandmother would always change around her room, and she would mix paints because she was often dissatisfied with whatever color would come from the store. It was eye-opening to me that you could really curate a space in that way. And my dad, he was a truck driver by profession. But on weekends, we worked on construction projects; we would build garages and renovate the exterior of homes together. Then at night, he would play music as part of a band. So I was always surrounded by some form of art and creativity as a kid.

Growing up, I loved to change my room around, acting like I was on *Trading Spaces*. After a while, my mom told me that the next time that I painted, it better be in my house on my walls. Ultimately, something hit me where I was like, *You know what? I think I want to do this for a living.*

After nixing architecture as a field of study because of the math aspect, I moved to interior design. I deviated from my creative path and went corporate for a while, but I knew I wanted to create spaces. Then in 2020, the pandemic hit and I was like, *Let's open a business!*

The Ankara Discs on the ceiling mirror the curves of the rug and leave white walls feeling anything but boring.

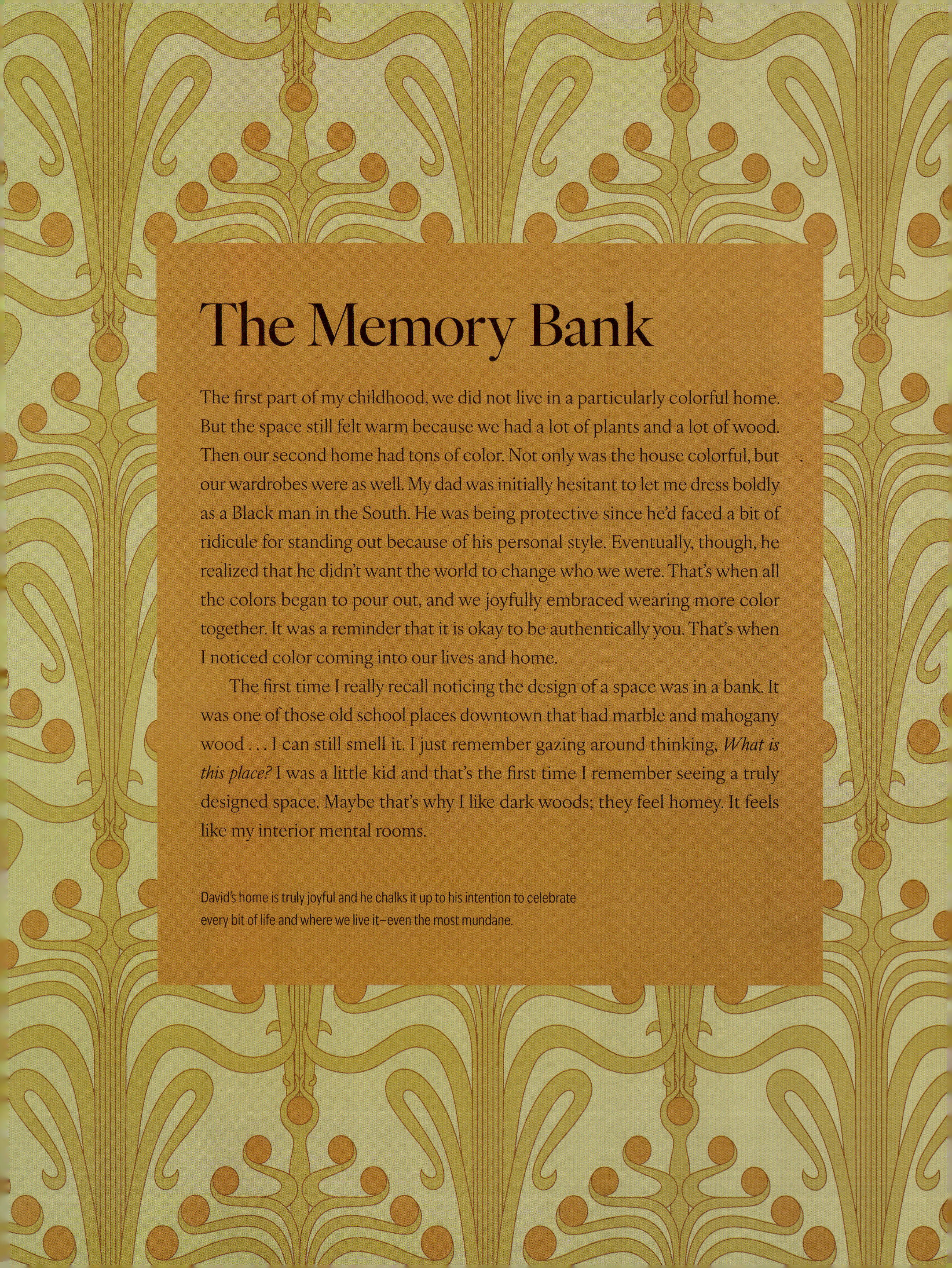

# The Memory Bank

The first part of my childhood, we did not live in a particularly colorful home. But the space still felt warm because we had a lot of plants and a lot of wood. Then our second home had tons of color. Not only was the house colorful, but our wardrobes were as well. My dad was initially hesitant to let me dress boldly as a Black man in the South. He was being protective since he'd faced a bit of ridicule for standing out because of his personal style. Eventually, though, he realized that he didn't want the world to change who we were. That's when all the colors began to pour out, and we joyfully embraced wearing more color together. It was a reminder that it is okay to be authentically you. That's when I noticed color coming into our lives and home.

The first time I really recall noticing the design of a space was in a bank. It was one of those old school places downtown that had marble and mahogany wood . . . I can still smell it. I just remember gazing around thinking, *What is this place?* I was a little kid and that's the first time I remember seeing a truly designed space. Maybe that's why I like dark woods; they feel homey. It feels like my interior mental rooms.

David's home is truly joyful and he chalks it up to his intention to celebrate every bit of life and where we live it—even the most mundane.

COOL
/KUL/
:YOU
CREATE

Art Today

# The Process

Growing up, when I was very down on myself or I let the world be down on me, I would create scenes in my mind where there was a space where I would allow myself to freely experience joy. And so I want to do that for people now: Create spaces where they always feel safe, loved, heard, and like their best selves. And what better place to do that than at home?

When I'm hired, clients know I am going to be their bridge to putting color and extra personality into their space. Some people definitely want wallpaper—it's nostalgic. They'll tell me about their grandmother's wallpaper or growing up with it in their childhood home. For others, I may shock them by proposing wallpaper, but many come around to it in the end. As designers, it is our responsibility to tell a client's story through scenery.

David's maternal grandmother was a passionate caregiver and David felt that the vibrant plants depicted in the print she inspired (Ruth's Garden) exuded a feeling similar to what she gave to others.

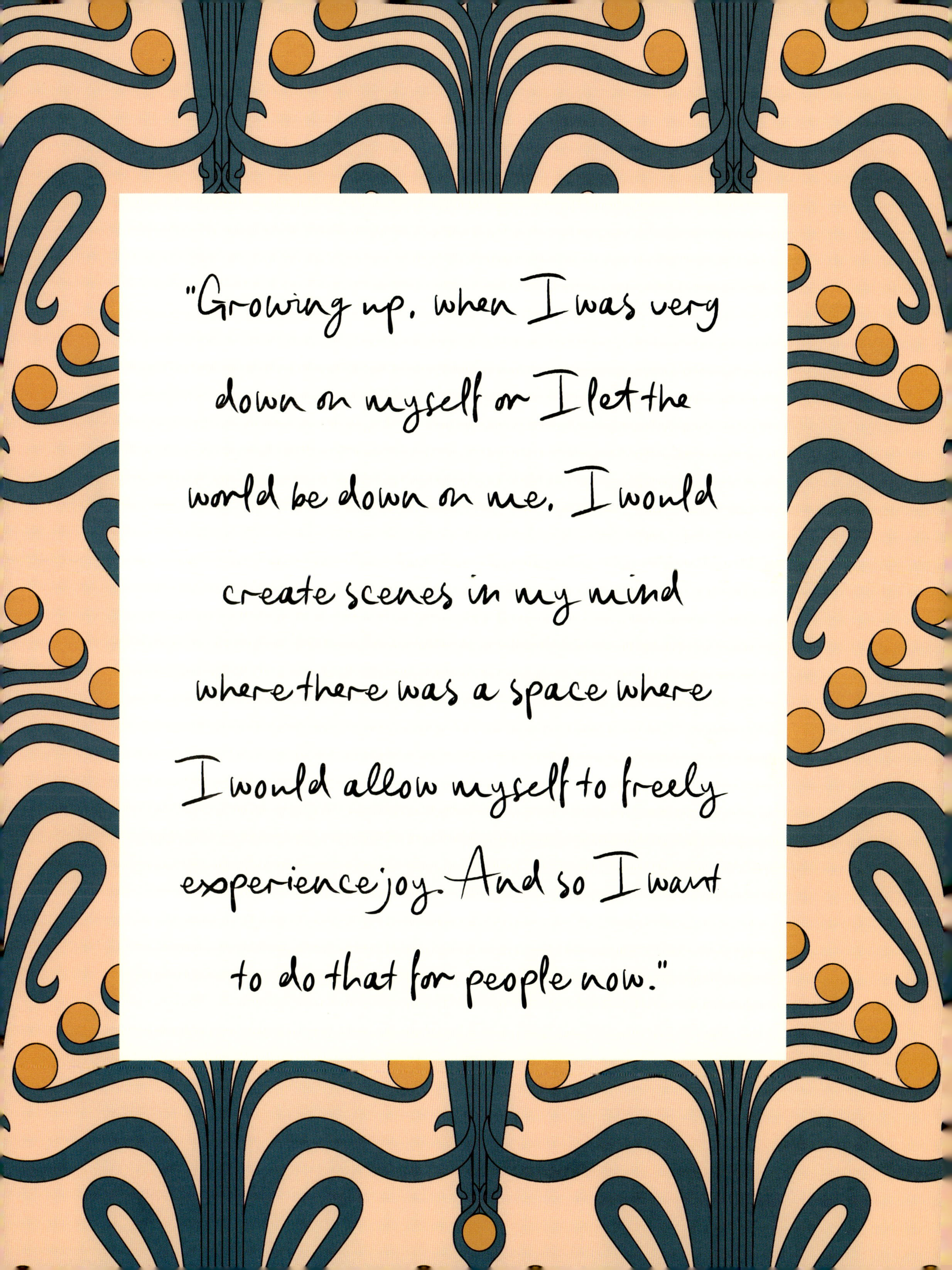
"Growing up, when I was very down on myself or I let the world be down on me, I would create scenes in my mind where there was a space where I would allow myself to freely experience joy. And so I want to do that for people now."

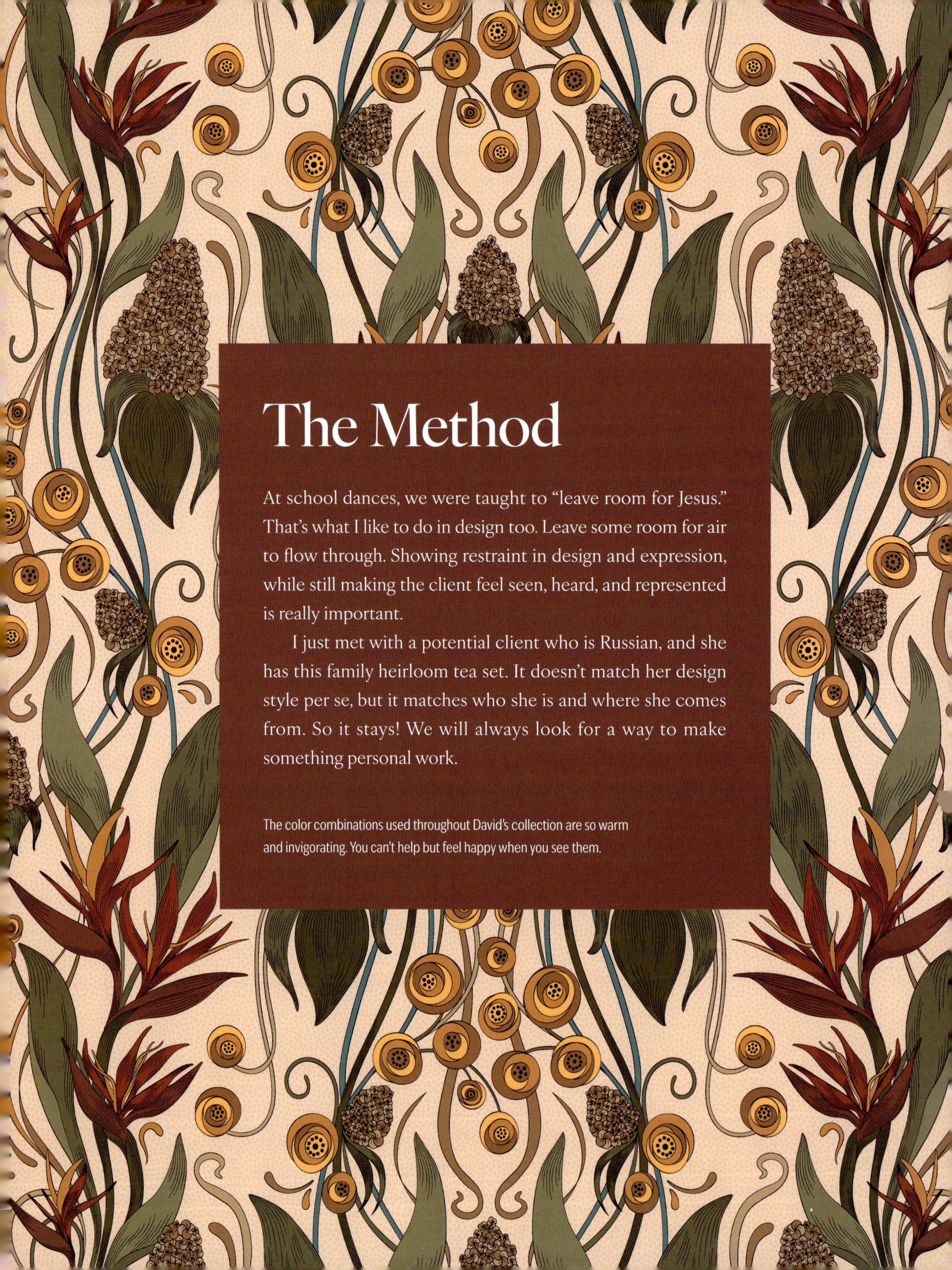

# The Method

At school dances, we were taught to "leave room for Jesus." That's what I like to do in design too. Leave some room for air to flow through. Showing restraint in design and expression, while still making the client feel seen, heard, and represented is really important.

I just met with a potential client who is Russian, and she has this family heirloom tea set. It doesn't match her design style per se, but it matches who she is and where she comes from. So it stays! We will always look for a way to make something personal work.

The color combinations used throughout David's collection are so warm and invigorating. You can't help but feel happy when you see them.

# The Inspiration

The matriarchs in my family were—and are—forces to be reckoned with. My grandmother Lucille always pushed me to be creative and the most *me*. As a mixed-race child with a Caucasian father, Lucille was hidden away whenever they had company. She later said that she never wanted to see or make anyone feel like that. So my admiration of her morphed into this ponderosa pine–inspired design for my line with Chasing Paper. Lucille was also of Caribbean and Creole heritage, and the design is kind of art nouveau. Ponderosa pines develop these beautiful nodes as they age, and Lucille aged so beautifully. Plus, she had twenty kids, so those nodes on the design also represent all of my aunts and uncles.

My mom's mom, Ruth, was the sweet one—but don't cross her! She was the one who always wore flowers and had the most bespoke hats in church. She loved on people and was like the neighborhood mom. They were from Orange Mound in Memphis, which is the oldest black neighborhood in the United States. I never got a chance to meet her, but my mom is very much a representation of her—not only in how she looks but also from the stories that I hear. So, in her honor, I created the design Ruth's Garden. You go into a garden to feel refreshed and rejuvenated, and that's what she did for a lot of people in the neighborhood.

David says our bedroom should give us a sense of safety and calm and be a refuge where we can recharge our joy. So incorporate all the details that feel most joyful to you.

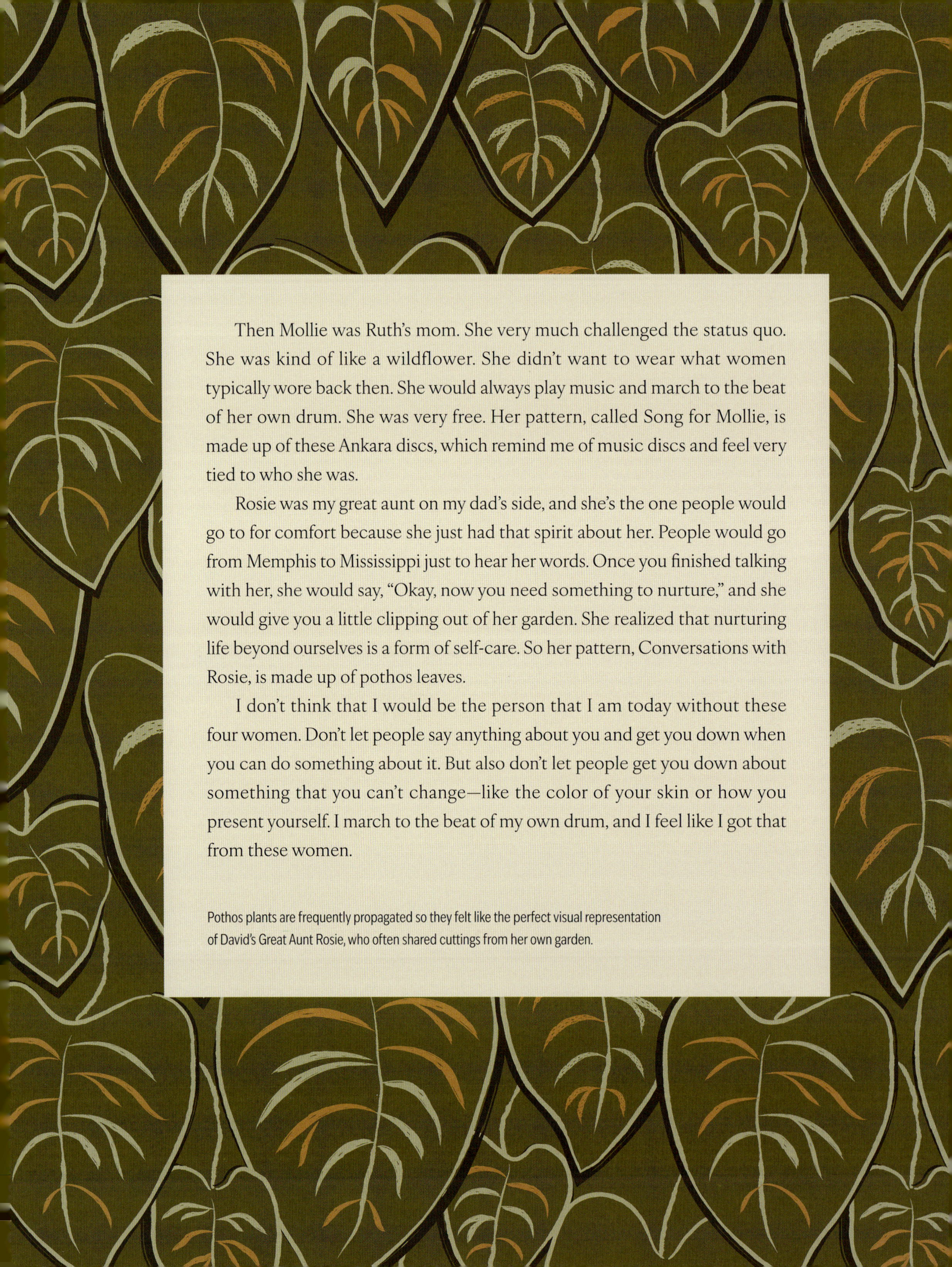

Then Mollie was Ruth's mom. She very much challenged the status quo. She was kind of like a wildflower. She didn't want to wear what women typically wore back then. She would always play music and march to the beat of her own drum. She was very free. Her pattern, called Song for Mollie, is made up of these Ankara discs, which remind me of music discs and feel very tied to who she was.

Rosie was my great aunt on my dad's side, and she's the one people would go to for comfort because she just had that spirit about her. People would go from Memphis to Mississippi just to hear her words. Once you finished talking with her, she would say, "Okay, now you need something to nurture," and she would give you a little clipping out of her garden. She realized that nurturing life beyond ourselves is a form of self-care. So her pattern, Conversations with Rosie, is made up of pothos leaves.

I don't think that I would be the person that I am today without these four women. Don't let people say anything about you and get you down when you can do something about it. But also don't let people get you down about something that you can't change—like the color of your skin or how you present yourself. I march to the beat of my own drum, and I feel like I got that from these women.

Pothos plants are frequently propagated so they felt like the perfect visual representation of David's Great Aunt Rosie, who often shared cuttings from her own garden.

COMPLETE BOOK OF
FRESH WATER FISHING

it was all
a dream

# The Crystal Ball

For the modern world, the pandemic was one of the worst things we went through collectively. Now I think people are prioritizing joy. Wallpaper is a catalyst of joy. You feel different whenever there's wallpaper—at least I do. Clients no longer want their space just to look designed, they also want to live and participate in the design.

David creates unique spaces through thoughtful layering, balance, and rich textures.

Susana
Simonpietri

**Susana Simonpietri**
**Brooklyn, NY**

# Meet Susana

**SUSANA SIMONPIETRI** *has always been a fearless adventurer in search of her next adrenaline rush. From appointing herself leader of the pack as a child to embarking on flying lessons as a mother of two, Susana draws inspiration from the surroundings she itches to explore. Born in Puerto Rico, she studied in England and Paris before earning her master's degree in interior architecture from the Pratt Institute in New York City. In 2009, she started her Brooklyn-based interior design studio, Chango & Co., which is known for creating everything from dreamy minimalist designs to energetic kid spaces.*

Started as a simple thread sketch

**HOW WE MET**

Susana is a true inspiration. Beyond being an incredible designer and creative mind, Susana leads her team with such warmth, compassion, and humor. Watching her work, I was absolutely taken with the way the Chango team brought children's spaces to life in a way that was imaginative, colorful, and thoughtful. Plus, they almost *always* included wallpaper! When we finally connected, it was incredibly fulfilling to watch Susana and her team dream up a wallpaper collection through iterative, experimental, and creative play.

Head in the clouds

Adventure awaits

DOUBLEDAY
GORDON
HERMAN AND ROSIE
REX/ROBINSON
SCHOOL'S FIRST DAY OF SCHOOL
Gaston
YOUNG FRANK ARCHITECT
FRANK VIVA

# Fueled by Adventure

I was a very active kid with an active imagination, and I took such pleasure in encouraging friends to join in on the fun. In fact, a friend of my mom was an artist, and she drew a young version of me doing just that. I have it on my desk now. Exciting others with an idea and initiating a plan to get people up and going has always motivated me.

I was a wild child. I practically broke every bone in my body, jumping and running around. Why live life the boring route? When you start having adventures, you see the world from a different angle.

The Chango & Co. collection is youthful and whimsical, but versatile enough to be used outside of solely kid spaces. A different colorway can transform the entire feeling of a print.

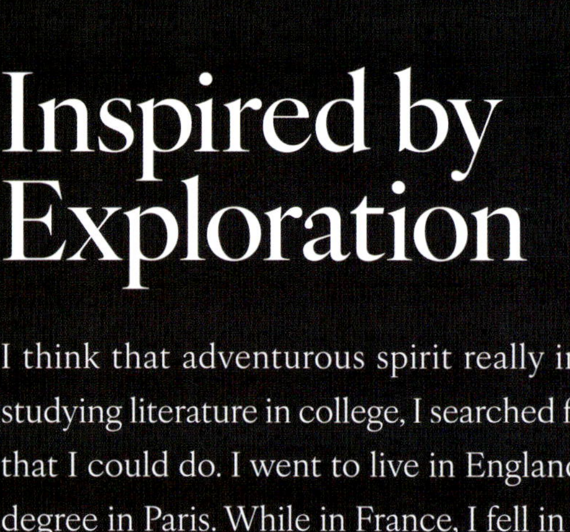

# Inspired by Exploration

I think that adventurous spirit really influenced my future. While studying literature in college, I searched for all the exchange programs that I could do. I went to live in England for a year then finished my degree in Paris. While in France, I fell in love with design and started to realize how important aesthetics are to the people there.

I had little exposure to the idea of design as a career when I was growing up, but once I realized that *design* had a name and could be part of everyday life, I changed my course.

Susana wanted to fill a void in the market with her collection, offering styles the team craved, but found didn't exist yet. Every print in the Chango & Co. collection is woven together with a unique stitch motif.

# Drawn to Design

I don't have a lot of memories of events from my childhood, but I have vivid memories of spaces. I could tell you exactly what my house in Puerto Rico looked like and draw a floor plan of my school. It's like the relationships and dynamics with other people meant less to my mechanical brain than the way the spaces flowed. That made more of an impression on me.

My mom has always been cool and has really good style. In the '70s, my parents renovated and decorated their mid-century house. The powder room we used all the time had the craziest, most amazing wallpaper. It was a large-scale leafy print in metallic silver and metallic navy. I remember sitting there looking at this pattern and being like, *This is awesome*.

When designing kid spaces, Susana says she regresses back to her childhood self and delights in creating something that will let imaginations soar.

# Motivated by People

I get very excited by people, and I love to make people happy. So I try to understand exactly who I am working for and what they are going to like. How do we fix whatever is not working in their lives currently? And how do we bring the best quality of life that we can for their daily experience in their home? So that's the biggest motivator for me when I design.

When designing kids' rooms, I regress completely back into childhood. There's an opportunity to shape their imagination and to be present in their development on a daily basis that I don't take for granted. So I try to make it as whimsical as possible and be completely fanciful. I want their imaginations to run wild and hopefully that's going to shape them in a positive way.

Stitched stripes give a sense of movement and playfulness to the space, keeping them from feeling too serious.

LITTLE
YOUNG FRANK
NEW YORK

# Constantly Evolving

I get the itch to change my kids' rooms pretty often. Each time, I talk with them about what they want, and I really look forward to doing it more with them as they get older. They definitely have their opinions.

When I was maybe five or six years old, my room caught on fire, and I lost everything. So we had to start fresh. My mom and I turned redecorating my room into this thing that we would do together regularly—every couple of years or so. Some were better than others, honestly!

As the furnishings within her son's space evolve, this dreamy background morphs with it.

"Wallpaper is a little bit like scent—it leaves a mark on our memories."

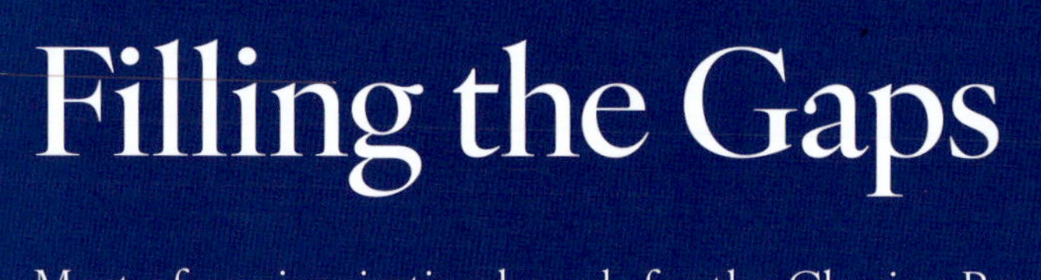

# Filling the Gaps

Most of our inspiration boards for the Chasing Paper collection were made up of art I had saved over time. And much of that artwork included lines that looked like stitching. So I realized that I was craving some sort of stitching pattern. I immediately got out my watercolors and started drawing. Then we sat down and thought about what the wallpapers we need are—the ones we're always looking for that don't exist. We ultimately used the stitching framework as the thread that weaves the whole collection together.

This Semi Stitched pattern is fully satisfying.

Ariel
Okin

**Ariel Okin**
**New York City, NY**

# Meet Ariel

*While* **ARIEL OKIN** *may not have followed a traditional path into interior design, she now has two feet firmly planted in the industry and a clear vision for her designs. Ariel first pursued a career in politics before realizing that her passion lies in interiors. Inspired by classic chinoiserie styles and Slim Aarons photography, Ariel incorporates these elements (and more) into her creations, leading to spaces that feel elegant, layered, and downright delightful.*

*Chinoiserie*

**HOW WE MET**

When Ariel and I initially connected, we were both preparing to welcome our first daughters, but I had been familiar with her work for years. On our first call, I was blown away by how humble, grounded, and warm Ariel was—especially for a woman whose career was soaring to new heights every year. Something I have always admired about Ariel is her pattern play: her designs are filled with color, texture, and playful details that make each space one that I reference again and again. Her work is rooted in nostalgic nods and traditional design principles, but still incorporates modern flourishes that make it feel current and accessible.

*Traditional with a twist*

Classic and considered

P
L

A
Y

Cecily Parsley's Nursery Rhymes
Warne
Appley Dapply's Nursery Rhymes
Warne
The Story of Miss Moppet
Warne
The Story of A Fierce Bad Rabbit
Warne
The Tale of Little Pig Robinson
Warne
The Tale of Ginger and Pickles
Warne
The Tale of The Pie and The Patty Pan
Warne
The Tale of Samuel Whiskers
Warne

# Planting the Seed

As a kid, I was always into something creative—I loved painting, drawing, pottery. My parents completely fostered my love for the arts and sent me to an art day camp in the summers starting at five or six. I was quiet and a big reader when I was young.

As I got older, I became more extroverted, but I was still very drawn to the arts and humanities. The summer before my senior year of high school, I studied photography in London and then I studied English literature and journalism in college. Art, reading, and writing were always huge influences for me.

I wanted to be a fashion designer when I was little. I would draw dresses over and over in my Lisa Frank notebooks, and I used to sneak *Vogue* into homeroom in middle school and read it inside my textbook. I think my eleven-year-old self would be really proud of where I ended up, though.

Ariel's signature style is classic and considered, and her wallpaper collection feels like a nod to the past while bringing her own unique perspective.

# Forging a Path

After going to grad school for strategic communications with a focus on public affairs, I was working in politics and then education. Still, my friends would come over to my apartment and say, "I'm moving in with my boyfriend. Can you help us decorate our new place to be more like yours?" or "I'm moving into a studio by myself, can you help me?" and it sort of snowballed from there. I realized I was spending more time on these free design presentations for friends than I was on anything else—and I felt lit up working on them.

As a kid, my mom used to take me to Barnes & Noble to relax together, and I would sit on the floor of the art section looking at coffee-table books. I used to pour over the interiors of the Slim Aarons books. I think that was an initial pull toward design that I didn't even realize at the time.

Wallpaper doesn't always have to be the main feature in a room. This papered closet offers a surprise pop of pattern that beautifully accents the space.

# Memory Lane

I can vividly remember what my nursery looked like in the first house we ever lived in. It was done in primary-colored stripes, and there were tiny little clowns on a horizontal border going across like wainscoting. (I think this is why I'm still terrified of clowns!)

We moved into our next house when I was about three, and my bedroom was covered in white wicker and pink and green chintz—a peak Laura Ashley/Pierre Deux/90s moment. My mom is an interior designer, so our homes were always extremely detailed and layered.

Ariel has always found inspiration in timeless designs—particularly florals.

# The Power of Paper

Wallpaper can transform a space more than almost anything else, barring architectural changes. We wallpaper almost every room we work on—it is so integral to the way we design. Even if we're looking for a solid in a space, we often choose a textured solid. It can make a room feel so much more finished and less one-dimensional. Textured or patterned paper gives a sense of heft to a space—it almost provides architecture when there isn't much there.

Natural motifs tend to make us feel at ease, so a botanical print in a social space is a no-brainer.

# Searching for Inspiration

I find inspiration everywhere: from nature to old interior design books and, of course, from our clients themselves. I like to build off of the clients' preferences and personal history when choosing wallpaper patterns. Do they like large scale? Are they into chintz? Do they want a more serene vibe with a solid grasscloth? Thinking about who our clients are as people and sourcing from there is really the key inspiration for us, because we want all of our projects to feel really bespoke and tailored to each and every individual. We once created a custom dining room wallpaper with a panoramic scene of Brazil for one of our clients. She is from Brazil, and it was so special to them to have that in their house!

I love looking at archival papers and different prints from different eras. It's so interesting to see how wallpaper has evolved and how the different printing presses and hand-blocking tactics have progressed into digital.

Have a favorite flower? Search for patterns that incorporate it literally or one that complements it and allows the bloom to be the star.

# Sage Advice

Home in on what palettes and patterns make you sing: Do you love florals and botanical prints? Do you like a geometric check? Are you a solid-yet-textured kind of person? Start there. There are so many choices on the market, I think it's important to really refine the inspiration images that speak loudest to you, and to dig deep into what, in particular, about those images you are gravitating toward and why.

If you feel most inspired out in nature, bring those elements indoors with your design. This soothing mural and floral bedding does just that.

# Brittany & Ben Hakimfar

# Meet Brittany and Ben

*The husband-and-wife duo behind Philadelphia's Far Studio,* **BRITTANY AND BEN HAKIMFAR** *are far from ordinary. Brittany worked for a number of prestigious designers in New York and LA before opting to move back home to Pennsylvania to start a family and her own design firm. She says her California-cool aesthetic is in demand from many homeowners in the area who are craving a change from the ultra-traditional designs of the northeast. After the move, Ben left his legal career to run the business side of the firm, and the two have never looked back.*

**HOW WE MET**

When I look at an image of a room that Far Studio has created, the design is truly enveloping—every detail seems to be well thought out. The mood Brittany is looking to evoke completely saturates the space. Similarly, when we collaborated to create their wallpaper collection, the duo's vision was clear from the start: They wanted something that told a complete story and felt like it all belonged together. Seeing the papers installed throughout their home, that story is rich, layered, and undeniably elegant.

Persian-inspired patterns

Subtle yet sophisticated
Tonal, moody, textured

# Family Influence

*Brittany:* I was the third child, and I like to think of myself as the "easy one." As the third kid, I followed things that both my older brother and older sister did. I was sporty and athletic like my brother, but I also loved fashion and things that my sister was interested in.

We lived outside of Philadelphia, but I am very thankful that my parents traveled with us from a young age. I got to visit these European countries that exposed me to different cultures and architecture and really shaped who I am as a person.

*Ben:* I am also one of three kids, but the oldest. My parents moved to LA from Iran in 1979 and abruptly started a new life there. We were part of a really strong Persian community in LA.

This Tonal Plaid print feels playful enough for kids and sophisticated enough for adults.

Lex

# All Signs Point to Design

*Brittany*: I was always very interested in the arts and architecture. My dad was in the business of developing hotels, so I was exposed to that world from an early age. By the time I went to college, I was sure I wanted to get into architecture. But during my undergrad at George Washington University, I realized that I actually loved interiors. I started working at a furniture showroom at the design center in D.C. and became familiar with different patterns and fabrics and really gained a background in the industry. I felt like everything I had learned so far was gearing me up for a career in interior design, and that was what I wanted to do. Ultimately, I worked for some amazing designers in New York and LA who really helped me develop my design sensibility.

*Ben*: For me, as the oldest child of immigrant parents, my career options were limited to attorney or doctor. I went to law school, but my path into the design world happened organically. My father was an antique dealer in LA, so I grew up going to auctions and estate sales with him. While I didn't enjoy it at the time, I find myself choosing to go there now. When Brittany started working in LA while I was practicing law, she exposed me to so much good design that I really started to appreciate it more.

As a late-stage convert to the use of wallpaper, Brittany wanted to incorporate tonal prints that offered more texture than bold pattern.

# Homeward Bound

*Brittany*: When I got pregnant with our daughter, I convinced Ben to move to Pennsylvania to be closer to my family. At first, I continued working for other designers, helped my dad with some hotel projects, and focused on designing our new home. I knew I wanted to start my own design firm, but I wasn't sure if I was the right fit for this market in terms of my aesthetic. A lot of people think of our area in Pennsylvania as very traditional and I have much more of a forward-thinking, West Coast vibe. But as I was designing my own home, everyone who would come over would be like, "Can you design my house?" I was at this age where my friends were moving to the suburbs and buying homes. So when I started to do my research, I found out that there was a void in the market here for anyone with an aesthetic like my own and that it was something that people clearly wanted. That's when I began taking on a few clients at a time.

I got very busy very quickly, but I'm not really business-minded. Ben is more adept at that side of things and had always been very interested in interiors and what I do; we have been together since college and he was always involved. It had been a dream of ours to eventually open up a studio together and flip homes. So once I started getting busy, we decided to go all in and do this together. He left working in law and took over the business side of the firm. All of a sudden, we were able to control our lives, and it was really an ideal situation.

Notice how the subtle movement in the tonal treatment on the walls gives the space dimension without distracting from the other elements.

ALEXANDER MCQUEEN: SAVAGE BEAUTY

"Wallpaper forces
you to step in and
take a closer look."

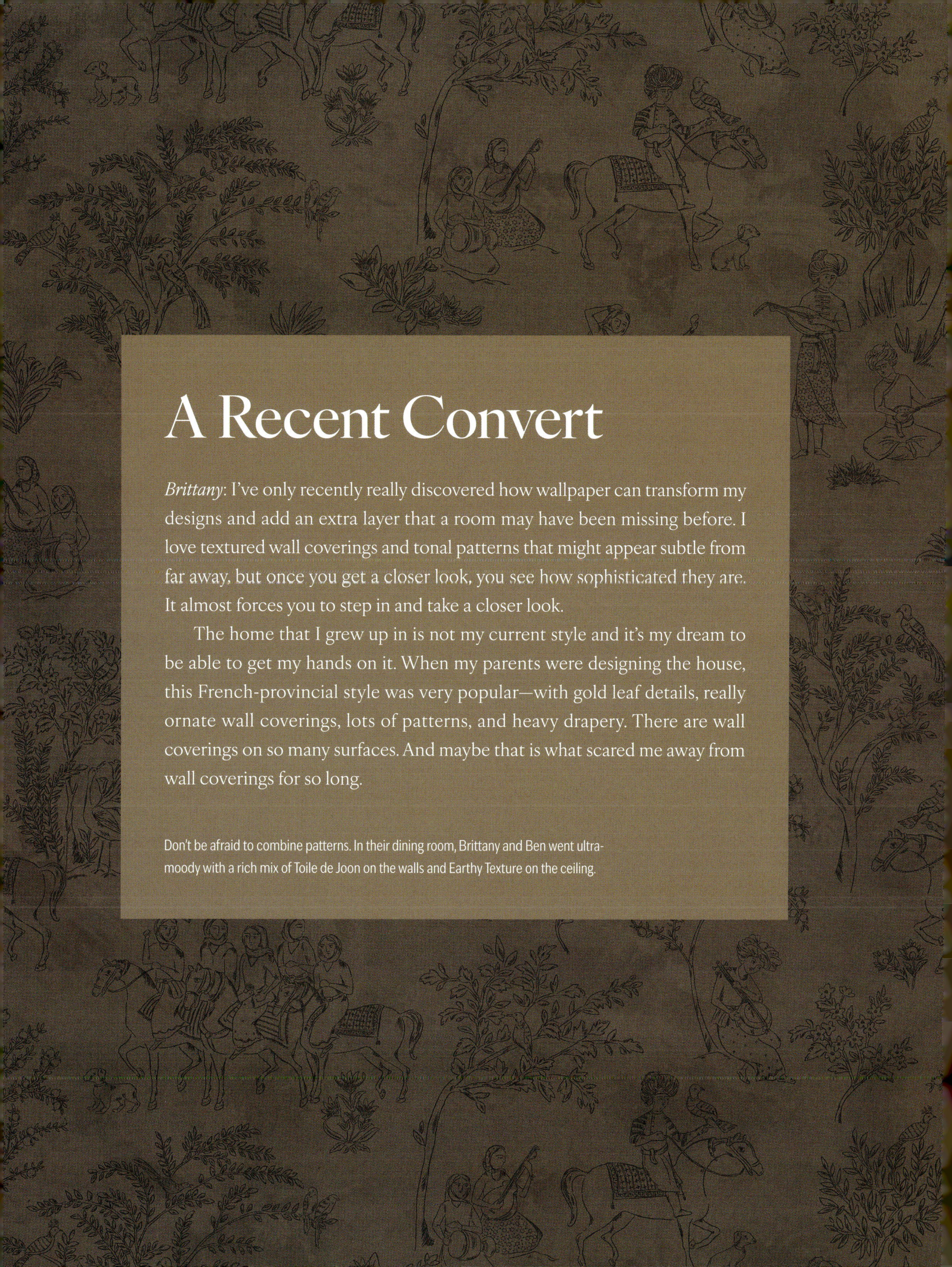

# A Recent Convert

*Brittany*: I've only recently really discovered how wallpaper can transform my designs and add an extra layer that a room may have been missing before. I love textured wall coverings and tonal patterns that might appear subtle from far away, but once you get a closer look, you see how sophisticated they are. It almost forces you to step in and take a closer look.

The home that I grew up in is not my current style and it's my dream to be able to get my hands on it. When my parents were designing the house, this French-provincial style was very popular—with gold leaf details, really ornate wall coverings, lots of patterns, and heavy drapery. There are wall coverings on so many surfaces. And maybe that is what scared me away from wall coverings for so long.

Don't be afraid to combine patterns. In their dining room, Brittany and Ben went ultra-moody with a rich mix of Toile de Joon on the walls and Earthy Texture on the ceiling.

# Dream Team

*Brittany*: When we were creating our collection with Chasing Paper, Ben was my sounding board from the very beginning. Pretty early on in the process, we decided to take Ben's Persian background and add that influence into some of the designs. We wanted it to feel sophisticated—inspired but not too in-your-face. We found an antique picture either from his grandparents' house or his dad's store that had images of Persian folklore, and it served as inspiration for our toile print.

I wanted to make sure our collection really had a cohesive feeling with really consistent colors throughout so it felt like part of the same family. We've ended up using it all throughout our home.

*Ben*: We actually want to add more. It gives each space an extra layer of interest and just looks so cool. Our designs feel classic, and I think they will stand the test of time.

Brittany's design style is all about the ideal marriage of hard and soft, masculine and feminine. Notice how the rough sink texture offsets the soft botanical print on the walls.

Anastasia
Casey

# Meet Anastasia

*Hardworking, driven, and full of vision,* **ANASTASIA CASEY** *of Austin, TX, is also one of the friendliest people you'll meet. Founder of The Interior Collective, a lifestyle site and corresponding podcast that showcases the best in interior design, Anastasia also does branding for interior designers. Moving to eleven new homes before college likely influenced her easy-going attitude, adaptability, and appreciation for the unique ways in which our homes can influence us. With a new baby in tow, Anastasia is tapping into those traits as she maps out her little one's dedicated space.*

## HOW WE MET

Anastasia and I were Instagram friends for years before meeting in person at a conference. She was exactly as I knew she would be: warm, effortlessly cool, and just as obsessed with design as I am. From there, we cheered each other on from our different corners of the internet. Later, while planning for Chasing Paper's next year of collaborations, Anastasia immediately came to my mind. We had such fun planning, sampling, and shooting together. Her use of texture in her own home and those of clients is a true testament to her deep connection to the world of textiles.

*Rooms with warmth*

English-inspired patterns infused with Texas grit

Mallorca

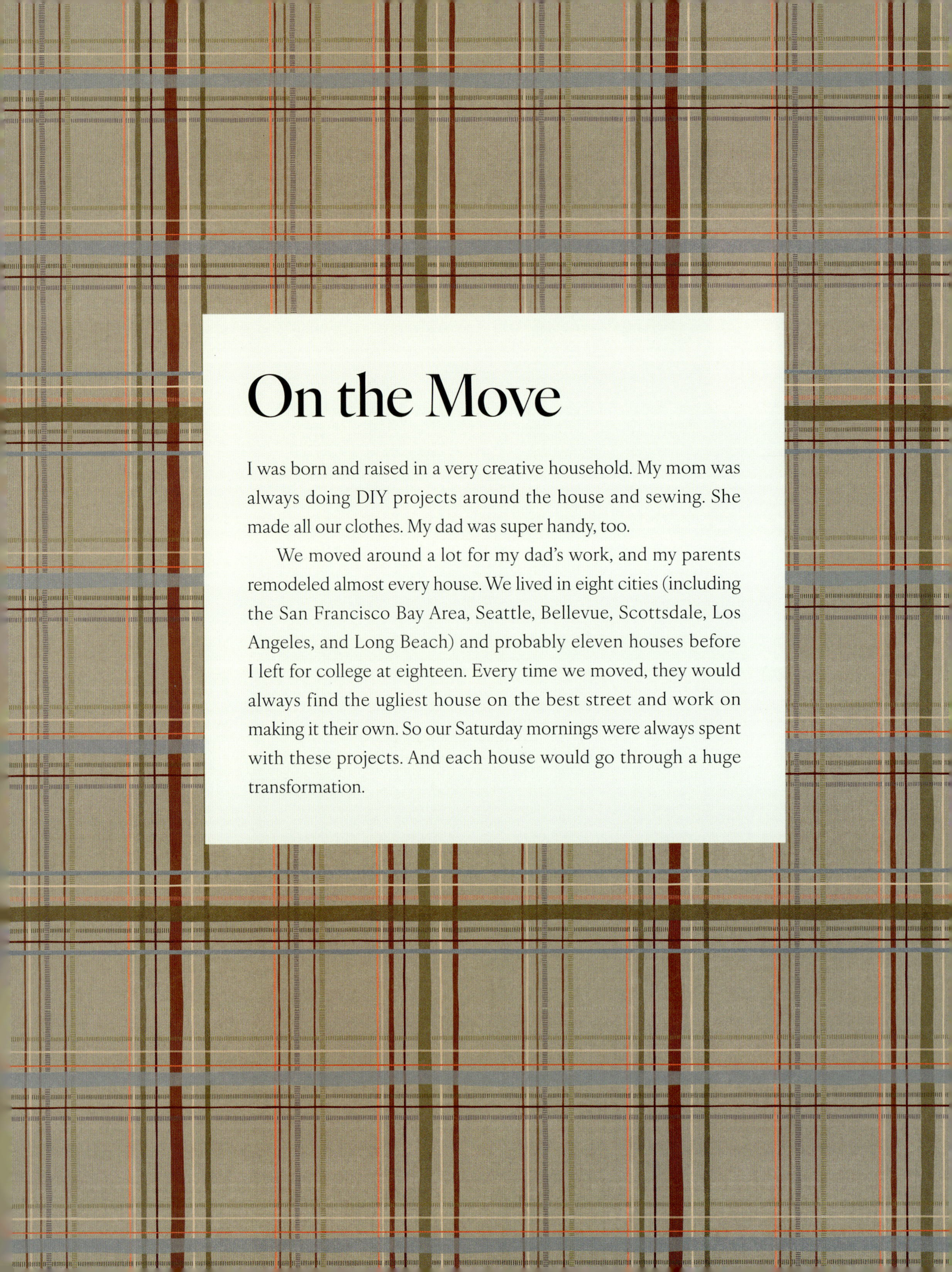

# On the Move

I was born and raised in a very creative household. My mom was always doing DIY projects around the house and sewing. She made all our clothes. My dad was super handy, too.

We moved around a lot for my dad's work, and my parents remodeled almost every house. We lived in eight cities (including the San Francisco Bay Area, Seattle, Bellevue, Scottsdale, Los Angeles, and Long Beach) and probably eleven houses before I left for college at eighteen. Every time we moved, they would always find the ugliest house on the best street and work on making it their own. So our Saturday mornings were always spent with these projects. And each house would go through a huge transformation.

# If Walls Could Talk

I can remember the first house my parents bought in Washington. I would have been about six months old, and we lived there until I was about four. That house was a beautiful butter-yellow color with ivy and rose wallpaper everywhere and poofy valances. It was the early '90s and in the height of fashion at the time, complete with white wicker furniture and patterned upholstery.

Any time we would move, my mom would paint murals for us. Our demands got more complex, so she'd sometimes use a projector to map out the wall. In Arizona, my sister was really into riding horses, so my mom painted a full-size barn with horses there. I wanted a Hawaiian room, so she free-handed palm trees that went up onto the ceiling. When we knew we were going to be moving to a new house, we got to start thinking about what our new room was going to look like. It was definitely a way of helping us feel settled and get situated. I hadn't actually thought about how the murals have shaped my love of wallpaper until now, but these murals were just a more affordable option for them at that point.

Anastasia says this bathroom didn't feel complete until the addition of the Posey Stripe wallpaper.

# Planting Roots

I was going to art school in San Francisco when I met my now husband, Quinn. We eventually got priced out of San Francisco, and we were ready for a little more space. Quinn also grew up moving a lot. He's lived in just as many cities as I have, so moving across the country was not scary to either of us. We started thinking about where we wanted to go. Quinn had gone to school outside of Dallas, but, being a California girl, I had never been to Texas. He told me to go to Austin to check it out, and we ended up moving there a few weeks later.

We were young and adventurous, and I think we could have been really happy in many other places. But we really found our groove in Austin. Our intention was to stay for two years, get a real job on our résumés, and go back to the Bay Area. Two years came and went, and we never looked back. Since then, we've convinced Quinn's brother to move here. My parents have bought a house here. And Austin has really become our roots. It feels like the perfect combo of small town and big city rolled into one.

A classic plaid alongside beadboard accents, rough wood floors, and crisp marble counters create a timeless and functional space.

VAN GOGH
MALEVICH
SUSAN WOOD
WOMEN
HERMITAG

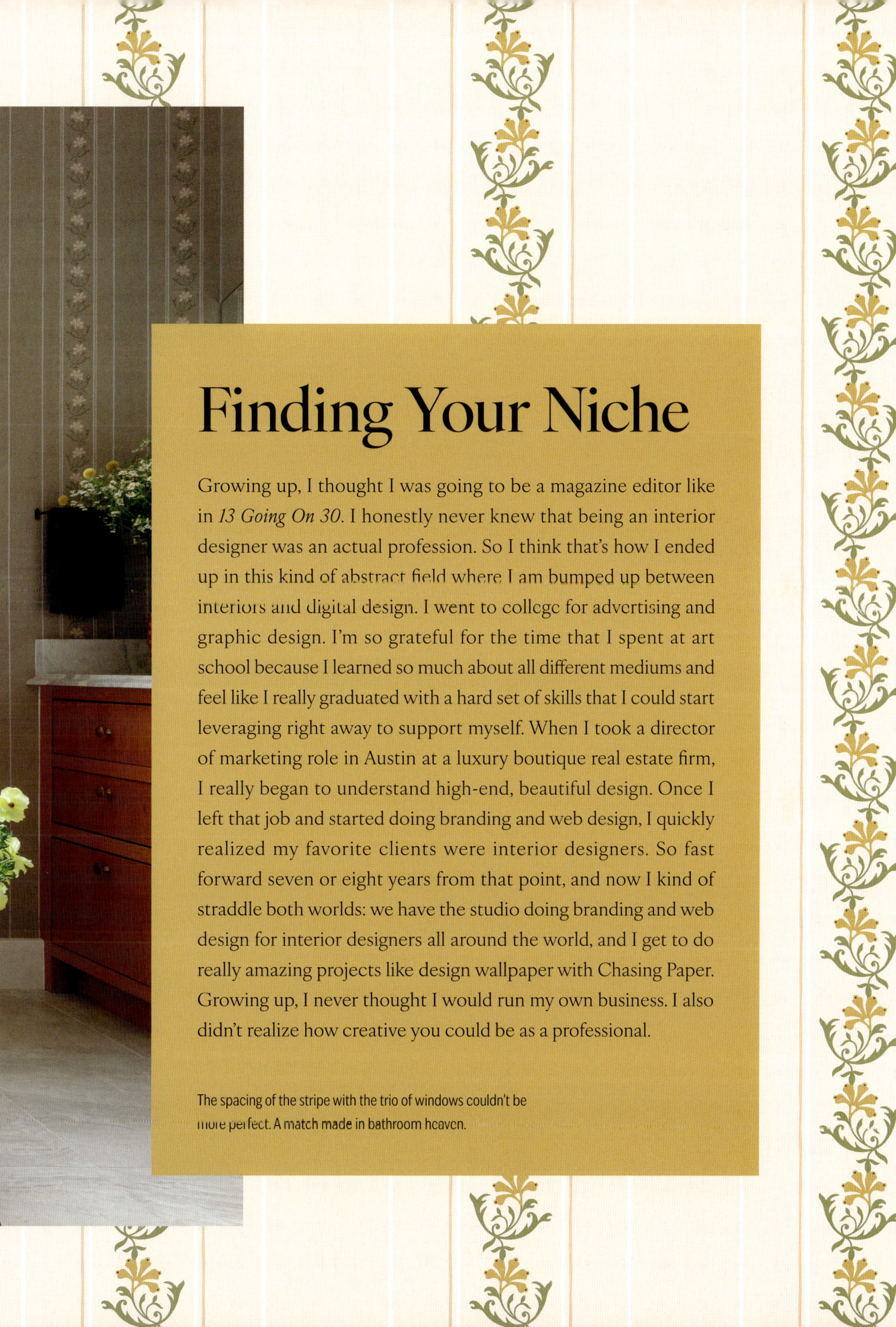

# Finding Your Niche

Growing up, I thought I was going to be a magazine editor like in *13 Going On 30*. I honestly never knew that being an interior designer was an actual profession. So I think that's how I ended up in this kind of abstract field where I am bumped up between interiors and digital design. I went to college for advertising and graphic design. I'm so grateful for the time that I spent at art school because I learned so much about all different mediums and feel like I really graduated with a hard set of skills that I could start leveraging right away to support myself. When I took a director of marketing role in Austin at a luxury boutique real estate firm, I really began to understand high-end, beautiful design. Once I left that job and started doing branding and web design, I quickly realized my favorite clients were interior designers. So fast forward seven or eight years from that point, and now I kind of straddle both worlds: we have the studio doing branding and web design for interior designers all around the world, and I get to do really amazing projects like design wallpaper with Chasing Paper. Growing up, I never thought I would run my own business. I also didn't realize how creative you could be as a professional.

The spacing of the stripe with the trio of windows couldn't be more perfect. A match made in bathroom heaven.

# Creating Character

Our first house was a townhome built around 2006. The previous owner had given it a very faux–Tuscany vibe with heavy drapery and iron work. When we moved in, I decided it was going to have the opposite: a cool, Scandinavian style with white walls and oak furniture—really clean and simple. In hindsight, though, I remember my mom being like, "Okay, but I think it needs a little more warmth." Part of my design decision was financial—that style didn't take a lot of layers or millwork. But then, as we would slowly save up a little bit more, I would scratch the itch and start another project. We ultimately added a lot of character to the house: shiplap in the kitchen, board and batten throughout many of the rooms, new stair railings, and updated bathrooms. I started implementing little bits of color into the once-neutral space. Eventually, we realized we'd done everything we could to this house and that we wanted more space for the family we were hoping to have one day.

We really wanted something historic, but that was not in our price range in central Austin. I found this house not too far from our office that had whispers of Tudor style and way more space. I decided to take it and really lean into the Tudor elements. Let's add character! I realize now that our old house, without the anchoring elements of color and texture, never felt fully complete. But here, I really leaned into the Tudor influence. The house and its bones will tell you the story that it's looking for. And nothing will transform a space like wallpaper.

This tone-on-tone stripe almost creates the illusion of fluted or beadboard texture from afar.

# Follow the Light

Light is something that I really take into consideration. Our nursery has one large window, but we have incredible trees outside. So it's not a very naturally lit space. Option A would be to put something in there that will lighten and brighten it. Option B is to lean into the fact that it's moody in there. So that's your starting point: do you want it to feel light and bright or do you want to create a *vibe* with a little jewel box of a space? From there, think about your furniture and think about what is going to be the backdrop to that and really make the furniture shine. If you have furniture that already has tons of pattern, you'll want to think about scale. Say you've got an amazing vintage floral sofa. Maybe you're going to want a smaller floral or smaller pattern to be the backdrop right behind it.

No matter what you choose, changing your wallpaper is really not as hard as everybody thinks!

Color drenching can be great, but wallpaper drenching is next level.

Fariha
Nasir

**Fariha Nasir**
**Austin, TX**

# Meet Fariha

*As a child in Pakistan,* **FARIHA NASIR** *was creative but never considered pursuing art as a career. Initially intent on going to school for economics, her plans changed and she learned to color outside the lines in the fine arts department. Fariha got married, graduated college, and planned to visit her husband in Houston, TX, when she found herself unable to travel back home because of a distrusting immigration officer. What was meant to be a two-month trip turned into an eight-year endeavor that ultimately laid the foundation for her DIY career. Fariha taught herself to use power tools to give her home the updates she wanted but couldn't afford, all while documenting the process on social media for family and friends. Her platform exploded and now allows her to give others the confidence to try their hand at home improvements.*

## HOW WE MET

What immediately drew me to Fariha was her fearlessness. She tackles projects with such creativity, thoughtfulness, and ingenuity while her audience (myself included) looks on in awe. When we were introduced through a mutual friend, I was immediately excited by Fariha's point of view and the ways in which she weaves color, pattern, and texture into each space she designs. Fariha is so kind and collaborative, and I truly believe that shines through in both her wallpaper collection and her client projects.

My Father's taste vs. mine

I like to color outside the lines.

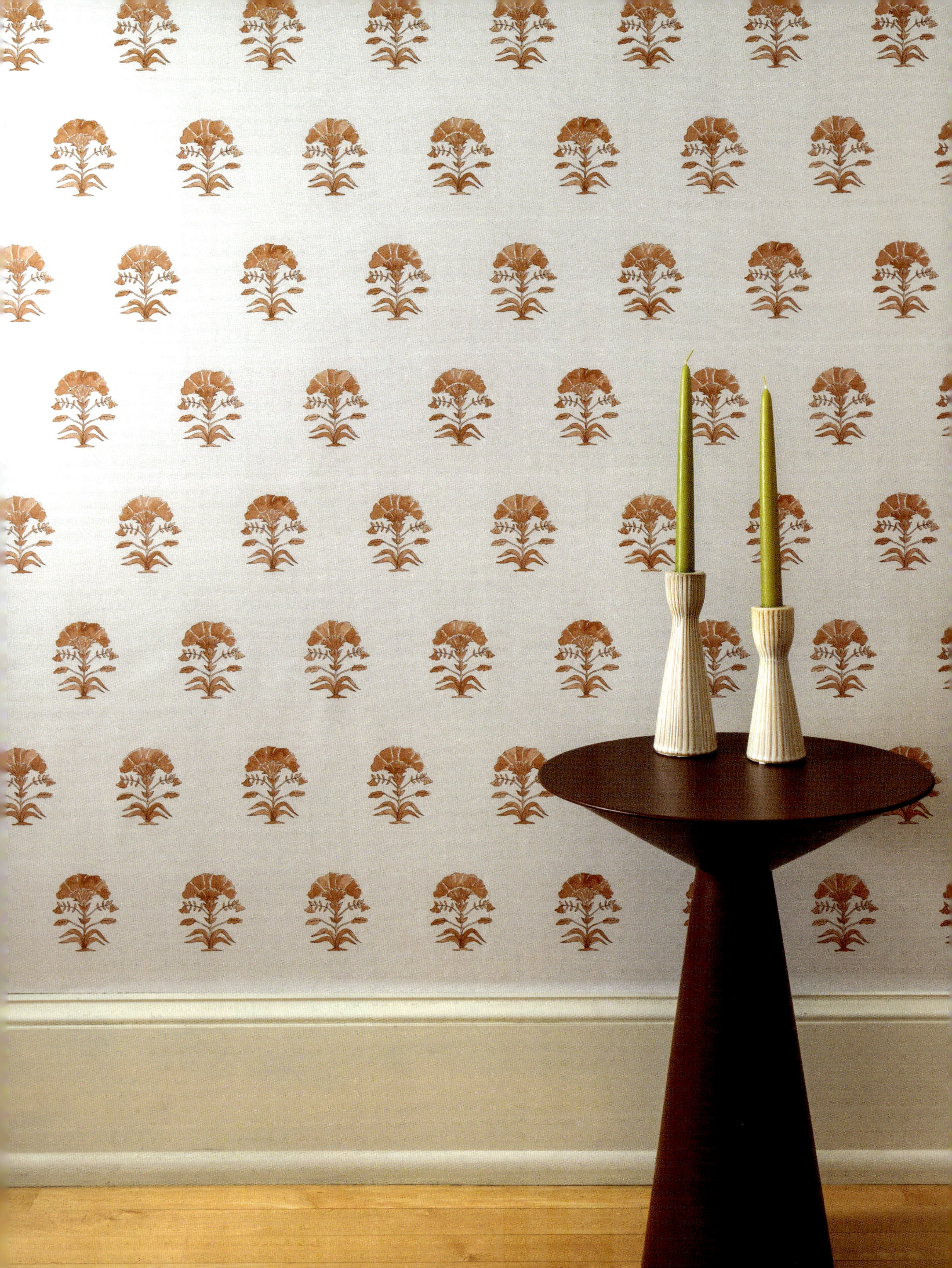

# The Makings of a DIY Darling

I was born in Karachi, Pakistan as the youngest of three children. My family has always lived in this one beautiful house that my dad built—he is very attached to this house. My dad and I don't see eye to eye on design. He went with white and crisp finishes and very traditional design elements. British colonial design greatly influenced the subcontinent and left a huge impact on everything from design to the way we speak. So, growing up, wallpaper was really reserved for commercial properties and held a functional role. It wasn't really something that you could go out and look for in stores.

I was always creative—I loved drawing and artwork and playing around with the interiors in our house. When I asked my dad if I could paint a chalkboard wall in my bedroom, it took him a year to come to terms with that idea. But after that, he let me do whatever I wanted to in my room. . . . except for painting the walls black. He drew the line there.

**Left:** Fariha's collection infuses her South Asian heritage into the prints. Block prints like this one harken back to her days watching her mother select similar styles in the markets of Karachi, Pakistan.

**Following:** Fariha creates a calm and serene breakfast nook with her Floral Garland pattern.

# More by Accident than by Design

When my husband and I moved into our first home in Houston, we never so much as made a dent in that house. We didn't even put up artwork because I was so scared to make any changes. The idea of customizing it was just so foreign to me that I couldn't dream of doing anything. In Pakistan, we have a culture of hiring everything out; we don't do anything on our own. There's no such thing as DIY there. And so in our Houston house, we just put furniture out and called it a day.

But after our first son was born, we moved into a bigger home. It was a builder-grade house, but I decided that this time I was going to make it my own. I thought, *I might not have the budget for hiring projects out, but let's see what I can do*. I started watching a lot of female DIYers on Instagram adding trim work and making furniture and I was like, *Maybe if they can do it, so can I*. I found a Facebook Marketplace listing for a miter saw in this shady-looking warehouse, and I bought it for $70. It sat in the garage for about a month before I actually tried to use it.

That first cut was so empowering and started my whole DIY journey. I began my Instagram account right when we moved in to document this process for family and friends. I had no intention of becoming an interior designer or an influencer or even monetizing these projects in any way. But suddenly my platform grew and grew, and my projects became popular. Then I ended up with two TV shows! Everything fell into place at the perfect time.

This diamond-shaped pattern is called *ajrak*, which Fariha's native province is known for.

PATTERNS of INDIA
Tale of the Tile The Ceramic Traditions of Pakistan
Mohatta Palace Museum

# The Presence of Pattern

Growing up, we had family in Indianapolis, so oftentimes we would travel there in the summer. It was very Midwestern. My aunt had this small cottage, and it had *so much* wallpaper. It seemed very foreign and interesting to me at the time. We're not new to patterns in Pakistan—we have so much print and color in our clothes. But I feel like all of the pattern is drained from our interiors and put onto clothes.

In my province, we're known for this pattern called *ajrak*. We'd use ajrak and block print for bedding, table linens, and clothing. Growing up, I remember going to markets to get our own custom designs made, and we sometimes looked down on that handicraft, thinking of it as so "traditional." I look back now and can't believe we had so many original handmade things that we never really treasured.

Pattern has always been part of my life, but I never imagined that it would translate into me having my own wallpaper collection one day. I think I naturally gravitate to patterns that remind me of South Asia. And so many of the English cottage-style patterns are inherently South Asian in my mind because of the British influence there. When designing, I try to embrace everything from back home as well as where I've been since.

The tones and patterns in Fariha's collection layer seamlessly together.

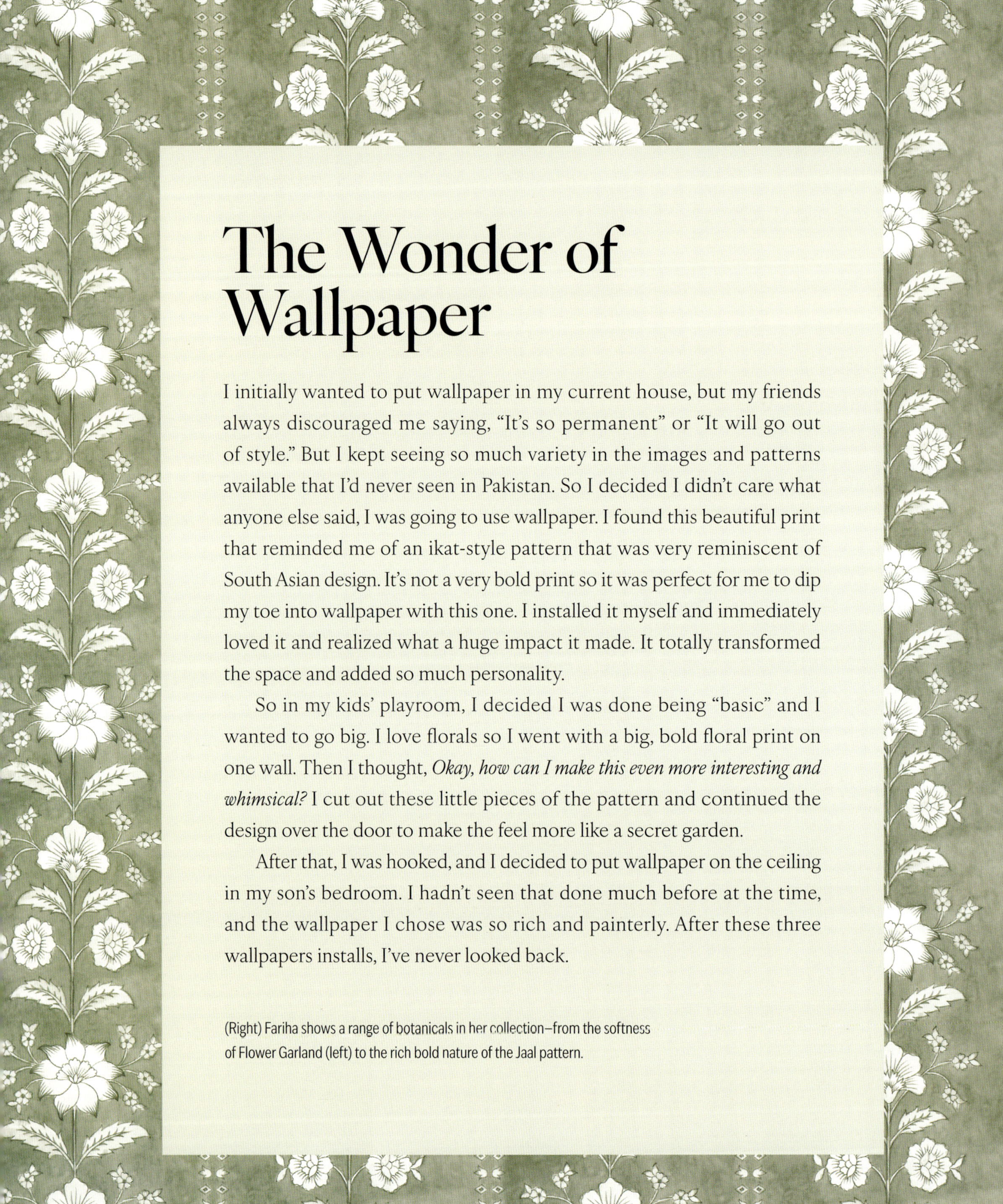

# The Wonder of Wallpaper

I initially wanted to put wallpaper in my current house, but my friends always discouraged me saying, "It's so permanent" or "It will go out of style." But I kept seeing so much variety in the images and patterns available that I'd never seen in Pakistan. So I decided I didn't care what anyone else said, I was going to use wallpaper. I found this beautiful print that reminded me of an ikat-style pattern that was very reminiscent of South Asian design. It's not a very bold print so it was perfect for me to dip my toe into wallpaper with this one. I installed it myself and immediately loved it and realized what a huge impact it made. It totally transformed the space and added so much personality.

So in my kids' playroom, I decided I was done being "basic" and I wanted to go big. I love florals so I went with a big, bold floral print on one wall. Then I thought, *Okay, how can I make this even more interesting and whimsical?* I cut out these little pieces of the pattern and continued the design over the door to make the feel more like a secret garden.

After that, I was hooked, and I decided to put wallpaper on the ceiling in my son's bedroom. I hadn't seen that done much before at the time, and the wallpaper I chose was so rich and painterly. After these three wallpapers installs, I've never looked back.

(Right) Fariha shows a range of botanicals in her collection—from the softness of Flower Garland (left) to the rich bold nature of the Jaal pattern.

# Lesson Learned

My advice to anyone these days is don't be afraid of adding wallpaper to all the walls. I know a lot of people say to start small, but I think if you're going to do it, do it all the way. Order tons of samples and trust your gut.

Another important lesson (I learned the hard way) is if you're having a hard time making a clean cut on your wallpaper, it's not you, it's not the wallpaper . . . it's the blade. Your utility knife is probably dull and needs to be replaced. I had the hardest time cutting grasscloth wallpaper recently and after a few panels, I changed the blade, and it saved me *so* much pain and frustration.

Stripes of varying widths combine into a print that could be confused with a textile.

# Acknowledgments

This book is a celebration of creativity, collaboration, and the power of design to transform spaces—and none of it would have been possible without the incredible support of so many people.

To my family: Your love and encouragement have been my foundation. Brian, you are the love of my life. Our life together is beyond anything I ever dreamed. Uma and Marlow, you are the best thing to ever happen to me.

To my Mom and Dad: Thank you for fostering my curiosity and supporting my creative dreams always.

To Katie, Annie, and Mikey: Thank you for being my cheerleaders and partners in every adventure.

To my team at Chasing Paper past, present, and future: You are the heart of this journey. Your passion, talent, and commitment brings every idea to life, and I am endlessly grateful for each of you.

To the designers featured in these pages: Thank you for your brilliance, your boldness, and your trust. Sharing your stories and work is a true honor. You inspire me daily with the way you see the world.

To Stephanie and Juree who helped me make the dream of a book a reality: Your patience and support are the greatest gifts.

To our customers and community: Your excitement and creativity fuel everything we do. Seeing how you transform our designs into homes, workspaces, and places of joy is the ultimate reward.

And, finally, to every person who believed in the dream of Chasing Paper from the beginning: Thank you. This book is a reflection of the magic that happens when we chase beauty and possibility together.

# Chasing Paper Wallpaper Index

# About the Author

In 2013, Elizabeth and her brother, Michael Rees, saw a gap in the market for renter-friendly wallpaper. As the third generation in their family's printing company, they had grown up learning the ins and outs of ink, paper, and patterns and saw their opportunity to bring thoughtful, design-conscious styles to every home. At the time, Elizabeth was living in New York City and had dealt with the common frustration and creative limitations that come with a rental apartment. Elizabeth and Michael began chatting about how they could find a solution to this problem. Pulling from their background, they created an innovative and superior removable wall-covering substrate to bring to mass and trade consumers alike. Today, the brand is best known for its premium wall-covering offerings that are used in a variety of residential and commercial spaces by interior designers, homeowners, renters, and more.

Over the years, Chasing Paper has partnered with numerous designers, brands, and creatives to bring unique perspectives and designs to premium wall coverings. These collaborators include Pehr, David Quarles IV, Hyphen and Co., Shadé Akanbi, Chango & Co., Jenni Yolo, The Interior Collective, and Ariel Okin. In addition to their best-selling collaborations, the brand also offers collections of evergreen prints that reflect their family heritage and legacy: wallpaper meant to be the backdrop of every family's most cherished moments and history.

Elizabeth holds a bachelor of arts degree in journalism from Indiana University and a master of arts from the American University of Paris, and resides with her husband and daughters in Milwaukee, Wisconsin.